GALTON

WITH

BY MICHEL

PHO

JOHN SCOT

*A seafood cookbook

HOOK
LINE
SINKER*

First published in Great Britain in 2017 by Face Publications.

Text copyright © Galton Blackiston & Face Publications 2017
Design & layout copyright © Face Publications 2017
Photography copyright © John Scott Blackwell 2017

A CIP catalogue record of this book is available from the British Library.

ISBN 9780955893056

Printed and bound in China

Written by Galton Blackiston
Foreword by Michel Roux OBE
Design & art direction by Anthony Hodgson
Edited by Jeannie Swales
Photography by John Scott Blackwell
Food styling by Tori Pearce
Prop styling by Angela Spruit Strid
Additional words by Chandos Elletson

www.facepublications.com

HOOK LINE SINKER*

GALTON BLACKISTON

*A seafood cookbook

COOKING IS AN ART A
CAREFUL SHOPPING FO
AND AN UNHURRIED AP
ALL YOU NEED. THERE
LOVE. LOVE FOR FOOD
THOSE YOU INVITE TO
COMBINATION OF THE
CAN BE AN ARTIST"

— Keith Floyd

ND PATIENCE A VIRTUE.
R FRESH INGREDIENTS,
PROACH ARE NEARLY
IS ONE MORE THING -
AND LOVE FOR
YOUR TABLE. WITH A
SE THINGS YOU

Like all the best recipe books, *Hook Line Sinker* is not merely a collection of recipes but an honest celebration of life, discoveries and ideas: a story shared about the simple, sometimes nostalgic, pleasures of sharing and eating. Few are so intimately and enjoyably written as this one by my friend Galton Blackiston. Having savoured so many delicious meals over the years, often with our fellow chef friends, at his beautiful restaurant at Morston Hall, I know this is the book Galton had to write. A gifted chef and gourmet, whose passion and forté is fish and seafood, here are recipes inspired by and featuring Norfolk's fantastic bounty served and plated in all its wild, briny glory – resistance is futile!

Most of the fish of the deep are celebrated in these recipes. It's a sustainable, seasonally available selection and it is heartening to find more expensive varieties, such as turbot and halibut, competing with their equally tasty yet humble cousins such as versatile little sardines, mackerel and brill. And there's an unashamed abundance of crab recipes: after all, Great Britain, and in particular Norfolk, must be the best place in the world to find and eat crab. Like British game, British crab is, in my view, the best in Europe, and widely exported yet so lacking in appreciation at home.

As if visiting his restaurant, here you are invited into Galton's effortless world with simple chapters helpfully named *Quick and Easy, Small Plates,* and *Stress-Free,* – and for when you feel like showing off a little, *Main Courses* boasts some real stunners. His recipes are irresistible, not only because they are delicious but because of his infectious enthusiasm, flair and delicacy of touch. Exceptionally imaginative, Galton is constantly thinking up new dishes and flavour combinations, but his discerning palate is that of a true chef, at once delivering the gentle charm of a beurre noisette but also the vibrant excitement of ginger-fried whitebait with wasabi and lime mayonnaise… even BBQ oysters! In fact, in giving my thoughts here, I find myself rewarded tenfold with his book proving an eye opener as I find myself inspired to tackle more fish on the barbecue. So I will keep a copy close to hand at my home in St Tropez, where I am so spoiled with the local fish markets and of course, in Bray at The Waterside Inn, with its supplies of daily fresh fish.

We are treated to *Hook Line Sinker* at this moment when Galton has something to say about his subject: a maturity and confidence in his craft. There is a glut of pointless cookbooks written by people too young or inexperienced but for him, the time is right to put into words what is natural, and I congratulate his instinct and sound judgement. As I do perhaps the most golden nugget of advice he offers that I want to endorse and finish on here, namely taking care not to kill your fish twice! The beauty is to find it served lightly undercooked, just slightly warm and pink on the bone, rather than white and steaming. Cooking fish is an art and in these pages, Galton shows you how to master it.

Michel Roux OBE

Foreword

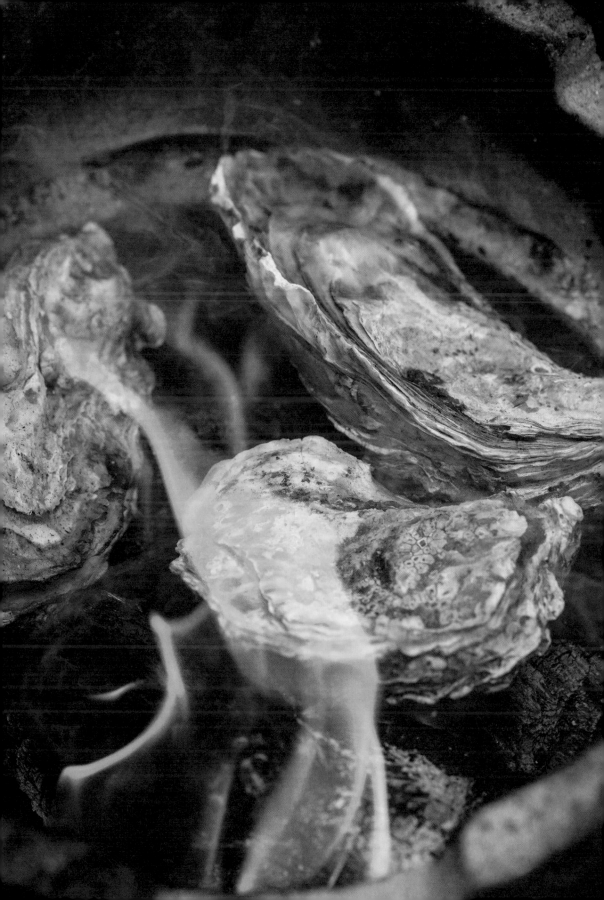

I WAS ASKE

WAS

RESTAURA

I WROTE

MY PASSION

AND FAVO

HOO

*By Galton Blackiston

INTRO-DUCTION*

THIS TO SHARE

FOR SEAFOOD

URITE RECIPES.

K LINE SINKER.

"WHEN I WAS GROWING UP WE USED TO GO ON HOLIDAY TO BLAKENEY IN NORFOLK WHERE WE'D RENT A PLACE IN AN ISOLATED SPOT ALMOST OUT TO SEA. IT WAS CALLED THE WATCH HOUSE AND THE ONLY WAY YOU COULD GET THERE WAS BY BOAT AT HIGH TIDE"

We'd hire a boat with a little outboard motor and take everything we needed for two weeks: all our food, sleeping bags, cooking equipment – you name it, it was in that boat. There was no electricity, so once we arrived we were fully self-sufficient.

I always spent my holidays there with a shrimping net at low tide, and trawling for cockles and sand eels. It was bliss. It was a haven for terns, so when we saw them diving for whitebait we knew it was mackerel time. The whitebait would jump to escape a shoal of hunting mackerel, and all we had to do was get a hook with a sand eel on it into the water, and we'd have a chance of catching a beautiful fresh mackerel. My mum taught me how to prepare the fish, and then we'd cook them over an open fire: it's where my love of cooking seafood began.

From there I steadily improved my knowledge through books, and with endless research and practice: I didn't have any formal chef training. My first job in a professional kitchen actually came about when we were on holiday in the Lake District, and the place where we were staying had a vacancy for a junior pastry chef. I took the plunge and applied. Before that I was running a food stall on Rye market selling pies and cakes.

When I opened Morston Hall in the early 90s I was still learning to be my own chef, and one night I came properly unstuck. The word was out about this upstart young chef who was doing something new in Norfolk, so I got a visit from a *Telegraph* journalist. The long and the short of it was that I got a proper slating in the press. The review focused on a strawberry garnish for a fish dish. I had a choice: I could either ignore it, or embrace it and start again.

I knew that I had to learn to trust my sense of style and cooking, and put myself on the plate, and that's what I did. To help me I bought every book written by Michel Roux and started to learn the classic techniques.

Back in the Lakes when I started out, we cooked salmon, lemon sole, plaice – pretty much the only seafood on offer. But today there's an amazing array of sustainable seafood in our shops and restaurants. People have changed, and so have their eating habits. In Britain particularly we're exploring new ways of eating, finding previously unheard-of foreign foods, tasting crazy flavour combinations, and then incorporating this melting pot of international cuisine back into our food.

Introduction

Introduction

Along the coast from Morston, we run No1 Cromer, a traditional British fish restaurant, which is always busy and shows me every day what a nation of seafood lovers we've become. It still amazes me, though, how many people – including professional chefs – have a fear of seafood. Perhaps it's something to do with the fact that it has to be fresh, needs to be cooked with precision, and there's little room for error. But, as with all ingredients, buy the right product and it's forgiving under the right circumstances. You just need to have a good seafood supplier and cook it well.

It's a fantastically versatile, healthy, delicious ingredient, whatever the occasion. The trick is to keep it simple and pay close attention to what you put with it. Trying out different flavour combinations, developing new pairings – that's where all the fun is for me! Throughout this book you'll find a diverse collection of ideas with influences from all over the world, and recipes with common ingredients that won't keep you in the kitchen for days on end.

This book isn't a huge how-to reference guide, or a seafood bible to teach you everything about each fish in the sea. It's a very personal book featuring some of my all-time favourite recipes, all of which have featured on my menu in some form over the years, but more importantly, are great to cook at home.

Seafood is one of the last truly wild sources of food on the planet. Even though fishing methods have changed dramatically, fish are still wild, living in their natural habitat, and are free to swim where they want and feed how they want.

I'm as enthusiastic about it today as I was as a child when I used to go shrimping and catching mackerel. I still get excited about really fresh fish, and my mind immediately goes into overdrive at the possibilities. I'm very choosy about where I buy my fish: the secret for me is finding a supplier you can trust. This might be a fishmonger on the high street or even an actual fisherman. You might find somebody at a farmers' market that buys direct from a boat, or you might know somebody at a supermarket fish counter who takes seafood seriously.

"I WISH YOU EVERY SUCCESS IN YOUR COOKING AND VERY MUCH HOPE YOU ENJOY THE RECIPES AND THE RESULTS. A LIFETIME OF COOKING HAS NOT DIMMED MY ENJOYMENT AND I HOPE YOU FIND THE SAME JOY"

BLUE
CRAB CL
HALIBU
LOBSTER/MAC
SALMON/SM
SCALL
SEA BR

*Simple everyday seafood

QUICK AND EASY*

BLUEFIN TUNA CEVICHE/
IBERICO HAM, AVOCADO, MELON & ROASTED TOMATOES

Serves Four

for the tomatoes:
12 cherry tomatoes, *sliced in half*
sea salt & black pepper
rapeseed oil

for the vinaigrette:
6 tbsp olive oil
2 tbsp red wine vinegar
1 garlic clove, *peeled, finely sliced*
30g shallot, *finely sliced*
90g very ripe tomatoes
sea salt & black pepper

for the tuna ceviche:
2 tbsp olive oil
500g fillet of bluefin tuna
sea salt & black pepper
juice of 2 limes
12 thin slices of Iberico ham,
or good quality Parma ham
1 really ripe Charentais melon,
peeled, thinly sliced
1 ripe avocado, *peeled, thinly sliced*
1 small handful fennel leaves

To roast the tomatoes, heat the oven to 100°C/210°F/gas mark ¼. Place the tomatoes onto a baking tray, season with salt and freshly ground black pepper and drizzle with a good helping of rapeseed oil. Place in the oven for 1¼ hours – the tomatoes will shrivel slightly and the flavour will intensify. Remove from the oven and set aside to cool.

To make the vinaigrette, place all the ingredients into a blender, season with salt and freshly ground black pepper and whizz for about 30 seconds. Check the seasoning and set aside.

To make the tuna ceviche, heat the olive oil in a frying pan over a high heat, then add the tuna and seal for about 30 seconds on each side, season with salt and freshly ground black pepper and remove from the pan to cool. When cool, slice the tuna into 1cm thick slices, squeeze over the lime juice and add a good pinch of sea salt, cover and refrigerate for 1 hour.

To serve, place the ham, melon, avocado, tuna, and roasted tomatoes onto serving plates. Drizzle with the vinaigrette and garnish with fennel leaves.

Quick and easy

ROAST COD/
GRILLED AUBERGINE & FETA WITH ROASTED TOMATOES

To roast the tomatoes, preheat the oven to 120°C/250°F/gas mark ½. Mix all the ingredients together, season with salt and freshly ground pepper, and spread evenly over a baking tray. Place into the oven and cook for 1 hour, by which time the moisture will have evaporated and the tomatoes will have started to dry out a little and colour. Remove from the oven and set aside.

To grill the aubergine, preheat the grill to high. Slice the aubergines in half lengthways, score the flesh and place onto a baking tray. Drizzle with 4 tablespoons of olive oil and season with salt and freshly ground black pepper. Grill the aubergines for 20 minutes, turning every 5 to 7 minutes, until evenly cooked with charred skin and the flesh feels soft.

Mix the garlic, parsley and 6 tablespoons of olive oil and spread over the aubergines. Season lightly with salt and freshly ground pepper, then crumble the feta cheese over the top, drizzle a little more olive oil, cover, and keep them warm.

To roast the cod, preheat the oven to 200°C/400°F/gas mark 6. Lightly oil a baking tray and place the 4 fillets of cod on it. Brush the fillets with olive oil and season with sea salt and freshly ground pepper. Place the baking tray into the centre of the oven and cook for 6 minutes or until the flesh just starts to pull away when pressed.

Serve with the grilled aubergine and feta, and garnish with the roasted tomatoes and lemon juice squeezed over the top.

Serves Four

for the tomatoes:
12 cherry tomatoes, *sliced in half*
55ml sunflower oil
2 shallots, *peeled, finely sliced*
1 garlic clove, *peeled, grated*
1 sprig of fresh thyme
1 tbsp vinegar
1 pinch of soft brown sugar
sea salt & black pepper

for the aubergine:
2 aubergines
extra virgin olive oil
sea salt & black pepper
2 garlic cloves, *peeled, finely sliced*
1 handful parsley leaves, *finely chopped*
150g feta cheese

for the cod:
4 fillets cod, *skin removed*
olive oil
sea salt & black pepper
1 lemon, *freshly squeezed*

CRAB CLAW TEMPURA/ LIME MAYONNAISE

To make the mayonnaise, place 2 tablespoons of the lime juice into the bowl of a food processor with the white wine vinegar, egg and mustard powder. Season well with salt and freshly ground pepper, then whizz on a high speed until all the ingredients are combined. Slowly drizzle in the sunflower oil with the processor still running; the mixture will emulsify and gradually thicken. Add the lime zest and more lime juice if necessary. Check the seasoning and refrigerate until ready to use.

Serves Four

for the mayonnaise:
juice of 2 limes, *plus zest of 1 lime*
1 tbsp white wine vinegar
1 egg
1 tsp English mustard powder
275ml sunflower oil
sea salt & black pepper

for the crab claw tempura:
300g gluten-free self-raising flour
1 small bottle of lager
1 red chilli, *finely sliced*
1 tbsp coriander, *roughly chopped*
sea salt
1 litre vegetable oil, *for frying*
16 crab claws, *4 per serving*

To make the crab claw tempura, place 250g of the gluten-free self-raising flour (gluten-free flour produces a very light batter) into a bowl and slowly add enough lager to make a runny, lumpy batter, with the consistency of thin cream. Stir in the chilli, coriander and sea salt and set aside.

Heat the oil in a deep fat fryer to 180°C. Lightly dust the crab claws with the extra flour and drop them into the batter. Lift them out of the batter with a slotted spoon and carefully drop into the fryer. Fry for 2 minutes, until they are crisp and light golden brown, and then lift out and drain on kitchen paper.

Serve immediately with the lime mayonnaise garnished with lime zest.

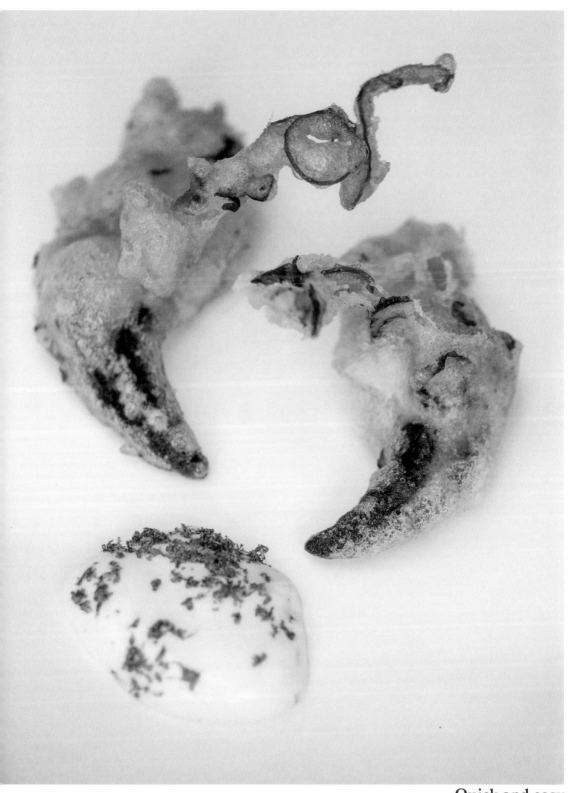

Quick and easy

SMOKED HADDOCK, PEA & LIME SOUP/
CHIVE OIL

To make the chive oil, blanch the chives for 15 seconds in boiling water, refresh under cold running water and then pat dry. Place the chives into a liquidiser, pour in the oil and blitz until you get a really vibrant green colour: the longer you blend it, the more the colour will be enhanced. Season with salt and freshly ground pepper, and pour into a container and set aside.

To make the soup, melt the butter in a large saucepan; add the onions and garlic and sauté to soften, then set aside.

Bring the stock to the boil, throw in 400g peas and 50g sweetcorn and simmer until just tender. Remove from the heat, add the mint leaves, and the onions and garlic and then blitz in a liquidiser. Pass through a sieve, set aside and cover with cling film until ready to use.

When ready to serve, heat the oven to 140°C/275°F/gas mark 1. Place the smoked haddock onto a baking tray and into the oven to bake for about 10 minutes; the flesh should be just starting to come away.

To serve, reheat the soup, stir in the cream, remaining peas and sweetcorn and check the seasoning. Ladle the soup into bowls and flake over the smoked haddock. Top with segments of lime and drizzle over some chive oil.

Serves Four

for the chive oil:
100g snipped chives
250ml of grapeseed oil
sea salt & black pepper

for the soup:
50g salted butter
2 medium-sized onions,
peeled, sliced
1 garlic clove, *peeled, sliced*
450ml chicken stock, *see page 236*
450g petits pois
100g sweetcorn
6 mint leaves
300g undyed smoked haddock
4 tbsp double cream
2 limes, *segmented*
sea salt & black pepper

PAN-FRIED HALIBUT/ BLUE CHEESE & PEAR SALAD WITH YUZU DRESSING

Serves Four

for the dressing:
4 tbsp yuzu juice
4 tbsp Chardonnay vinegar
½ tsp sea salt flakes
1 tsp red chilli, *finely sliced*
3 tbsp chopped coriander
200g olive oil
½ tsp caster sugar
1 tbsp mirin
sea salt & black pepper

for the salad:
2 heads green chicory
2 heads purple chicory
2 ripe Williams pears
150g Montagnolo Affine cheese,
or any blue cheese
4 tbsp surfine capers

for the halibut:
2 large halibut steaks,
each about 200g
rapeseed oil
25g salted butter
sea salt & black pepper

To make the dressing, combine all the ingredients in a bowl, season with salt and freshly ground pepper, cover and set aside.

To make the salad, separate the chicory leaves, peel and slice the pears and break the cheese into thumbnail-sized chunks. Place everything into a serving bowl, add the capers, cover and set aside.

To cook the halibut, heat a frying pan until hot, add a splash of rapeseed oil and the butter followed by the halibut steaks and fry for about 5 minutes, turning to colour well on both sides.

To serve, flake the halibut into the salad and drizzle with a good helping of yuzu dressing.

Quick and easy

LEMON SOLE FINGERS/
VIETNAMESE DIPPING SAUCE

To make the dipping sauce, gently heat the sesame oil in a saucepan and add the shallots, garlic, ginger and chillies. Stir well and sweat the vegetables over a medium heat for 8 to 10 minutes, until the shallots are soft. Pour in the mirin and increase the heat slightly. Stir and simmer the mixture until it has reduced by half. Add the sugar syrup, lime juice and vinegar. Simmer for a few minutes then add the soy and fish sauce. Taste and adjust the seasoning to your liking, adding more sugar syrup, lime juice or soy sauce as necessary.

Serves Four

for the dipping sauce:
5 tsp sesame oil
4 shallots, *peeled, finely sliced*
1 garlic clove, *peeled, finely sliced*
15g fresh ginger, *peeled, grated*
3 red chillies, *deseeded, sliced*
50ml mirin
3 tbsp sugar syrup
50ml lime juice
125ml rice wine vinegar
60ml soy sauce
5 tsp nam pla fish sauce
1 small bunch of coriander,
finely chopped

for the lemon sole:
4 lemon sole fillets,
skinned and cut into 'fish fingers'
75g seasoned plain flour
2 eggs and 150ml milk,
beaten together to make an egg wash
100g Panko breadcrumbs
1 level tbsp mild curry powder
rapeseed oil
1 knob of salted butter
1 lemon, *cut in wedges to serve*
sea salt & black pepper

Take the pan off the heat and leave to cool (if making ahead, pour the hot mixture into a sterilised jar, seal and leave to cool completely). Stir the chopped coriander into the sauce a few minutes before you are ready to serve.

To make the lemon sole fingers, cut the fillets into 'fish fingers' so that they're even in size – about the size of your index finger.

Use three separate bowls: place the seasoned flour into one, the egg wash into another, and combine the breadcrumbs with the curry powder and place into the third.

Next, quickly dip the fish fingers into the flour, pat off the excess before dipping into the egg wash, and shake off any excess egg wash before carefully coating with the breadcrumbs.

Place the crumbed fish fingers onto a tray and repeat with the remaining fish.

Heat a frying pan over a medium heat, add a little rapeseed oil and a knob of butter and gently fry the fish until coloured on both sides and the fish is cooked through. Remove from the pan and drain well on kitchen paper.

Serve immediately with the dipping sauce and a good squeeze of lemon juice over the fish.

LOBSTER CURRY

Serves Four

rapeseed oil

2 shallots, *peeled, finely sliced*

8 garlic cloves, *peeled, grated*

1 large lobe of ginger,
peeled, grated

2 tsp sea salt flakes

1 tsp ground turmeric

1 tsp ground cumin

1 tsp ground cinnamon

1 tsp chilli powder

400ml coconut milk

200g tomatoes, *roughly chopped*

300ml white fish stock,
see page 238

50g desiccated coconut

2 hot green fresh chillies,
finely sliced

juice of 1 lemon

sea salt & black pepper

the meat from 2 cooked lobsters,
cut into 2cm chunks

1 cauliflower, *broken into small florets*

250g paneer cheese,
cut into small cubes

6 tbsp fresh coriander,
roughly chopped

Heat a heavy-based pan over a medium heat, pour in a little rapeseed oil and add the shallots. Cook for 5 minutes until the shallots are just starting to colour. Add the garlic and continue to cook, stirring for a further 4 to 5 minutes – the shallots should be golden in colour by now. Add the ginger, salt flakes and all the dry spices, stir and cook for a further 2 to 3 minutes until the spices are fragrant.

Pour in the coconut milk, chopped tomatoes and stock and stir well. Bring to the boil and then reduce the heat and simmer for 10 to 15 minutes, or until the sauce has thickened slightly (don't worry if it looks split).

In a separate frying pan, dry fry the desiccated coconut until golden and then add it and the fresh chillies to the curry and cook for a further 3 to 4 minutes or until thickened. Season with lemon juice, salt and freshly ground black pepper.

To serve, add the lobster and cauliflower florets to the curry and make sure the lobster is warmed right through and the cauliflower just cooked.

Heat another frying pan, add a splash of rapeseed oil and fry the cubes of paneer cheese, turning to colour all sides lightly.

Finally stir in the fried paneer and chopped coriander to the curry and serve immediately.

Quick and easy

GRILLED MACKEREL/ GREEN BEAN, FENNEL & APPLE KIMCHEE

Although this is an easy dish, the kimchee should be made at least 3 days in advance: the longer it ferments, the more the flavour will be enhanced.

To make the kimchee, cut the cabbage in half lengthways, remove the centre core and then cut into small cubes. Do the same with the fennel, and top and tail the beans. Place them together with the grated apple into a colander. Sprinkle with the sugar and salt and mix well. Leave for at least 2 hours to draw out any moisture.

In a bowl mix the garlic, ginger, and chilli flakes with the fish and soy sauces and shrimp paste to make a paste. Combine the vegetables and paste and then place in a sealed container at room temperature for at least 3 days to ferment. The kimchee can then be kept in the fridge for up to 1 month.

To grill the mackerel, preheat the grill to high. Gently score the skin of the mackerel, brush with a little olive oil and season with salt and freshly ground black pepper. Place under the grill for 4 to 6 minutes – the skin should be crisp, starting to bubble and pull away easily.

Serve with a generous helping of kimchee and a sprig of coriander.

Serves Four

for the kimchee:
1 napa Chinese cabbage
1 bulb of fennel
100g extra-fine green beans
2 Cox's Orange Pippin apples, *grated*
120g caster sugar
3 tsp salt
10 garlic cloves, *peeled, grated*
1 large lobe of ginger, *peeled, grated*
20g chilli flakes
4 tbsp nam pla fish sauce
4 tbsp soy sauce
2 tsp shrimp paste

for the mackerel:
4 mackerel fillets
olive oil
1 small bunch of coriander
sea salt & black pepper

OYSTER TARTARE

Serves Four

12 oysters, *3 per serving*
5cm lobe of fresh horseradish,
peeled, grated
1 tbsp Chardonnay vinegar
2 tbsp crème fraîche
1 tbsp chopped chives
sea salt & black pepper
1 lemon, *freshly squeezed*

Shuck the oysters and retain the juice and shells. Clean and dry the shells.

Mix together the horseradish, vinegar, crème fraîche and oyster juice in a bowl, and season with a good helping of freshly ground black pepper. Finely chop the oyster flesh and mix with the dressing.

Serve the tartare in the reserved oyster shells, and garnish with chopped chives, flakes of sea salt and a good squeeze of lemon juice.

SEARED SALMON SALAD/ CREAMY MAYONNAISE

Serves Four

for the mayonnaise:
3 egg yolks
1 tsp English mustard
1 tsp white wine vinegar
sea salt & black pepper
300ml light grapeseed oil
juice of 1 lemon
50ml double cream

for the salad:
rapeseed oil
2 red peppers
200g quinoa
100g broad beans,
or 60g podded weight
1 tbsp pumpkin seeds
1 tbsp sunflower seeds
1 preserved lemon, *finely sliced*
1 handful of fresh parsley, *chopped*
1 handful of fresh mint, *chopped*
20g clear honey
½ lemon, *juiced*
60ml olive oil
sea salt & black pepper

for the salmon:
300g fillet of salmon,
skinned, pin bones removed
rapeseed oil
sea salt & black pepper

To make the mayonnaise, place the eggs, mustard and vinegar into the bowl of a food processor, season with salt and freshly ground black pepper and whizz on a high speed intermittently. Slowly drizzle in the grapeseed oil and lemon juice: the mixture will thicken and emulsify. Scrape into a bowl and whisk in the double cream. Season again and set aside.

To make the salad, preheat the oven to 220°C/425°F/gas mark 7. Oil a baking tray with rapeseed oil. Cut the peppers in half, remove the seeds, place them cut side down onto the tray and drizzle with rapeseed oil. Place in the oven for 10 minutes, turn the tray around and cook for a further 10 minutes: the idea is to get the skins off without charring or shrinking them. When the skins are sufficiently wrinkled, remove from the oven, place into a bowl and cover with cling film. Peel off the skins, finely slice and set aside.

Place the quinoa into a fine mesh sieve, rinse under cold running water and drain. Bring a pan of lightly salted water to the boil and add the quinoa. Turn down to a lively simmer, and leave for about 15 minutes, until tender. Drain in a sieve and then cool under running water and set aside.

Place the broad beans into a bowl, cover with boiling water, stand for 2 minutes then drain. Take the skins off the broad beans and set aside.

Heat a little rapeseed oil in a frying pan and fry the pumpkin and sunflower seeds until golden brown and set aside.

Combine the sliced red peppers, quinoa, broad beans, preserved lemon, parsley and mint in a bowl. Pour in the cooled seeds and season with salt and freshly ground black pepper.

Whisk the honey, lemon juice and olive oil together in a separate small bowl, and season well. Drizzle over the salad.

To sear the salmon, preheat the oven to 100°C/210°F/gas mark ¼. Place the salmon onto a baking tray, drizzle with a little rapeseed oil and season with salt and freshly ground black pepper. Cook for 5 to 10 minutes: the fish should be translucent and only just cooked through.

Spoon the salad into the centre of each plate and flake over the salmon, drizzle with the creamy mayonnaise to finish.

"TAKE A WHOLE SIDE OF
AND COVER IT WITH S
24 HOURS AND THEN
LIGHT THE SMOKER AN
TEMPERATURE SET LO
FOR UP TO 12 HOURS.
TO 7 DAYS WRAPPED

PIN-BONED SALMON
ALT TO CURE IT FOR
WASH OFF THE SALT.
D WITH THE
W SMOKE THE SALMON
T WILL KEEP FOR UP
UP IN THE FRIDGE"

SMOKED SALMON CORNETS

For this recipe you'll need some metal pastry cornet horns for the pastry cornets, which can be made well in advance.

To make the cornets, preheat the oven to 180°C/350°F/gas mark 4. Lay 1 sheet of Feuilles De Bric pastry onto your work surface, brush with melted butter and cut out 3 circles to 7.5cm. Wrap each circle of pastry (buttered side against the metal) around a pastry cornet horn. Repeat this with the other 3 sheets of pastry to make 12 cornets. Brush the outside of the pastry with melted butter.

Bake in the preheated oven for about 10 minutes watching carefully until the pastry is golden. Remove from the oven and allow to cool before slipping the pastry cornet off the metal horn. Store in an airtight container until needed.

To make the filling, finely chop the salmon into small dice, place in a bowl with the olive oil and lime juice, season with salt and freshly ground black pepper and combine. Cover with cling film and refrigerate until ready to use.

To serve, fill the bottom half of each cornet with seasoned crème fraîche, and top with the diced smoked salmon.

Serves Four

for the cornets:
4 sheets of Feuilles De Bric pastry
6 tbsp melted butter

for the filling:
250g piece of smoked salmon
2 tbsp olive oil
juice of 1 lime
sea salt & black pepper
4 tbsp crème fraîche

Quick and easy

Quick and easy

STRAWBERRY & LIME SCALLOP TARTARE/ BREAD CRISPS

To make the crisps, preheat the oven to 200°C/400°F/gas mark 6. Remove the crusts from the bread. Using a rolling pin, roll out the bread as thinly as possible – or roll it through a pasta machine. Using a 6cm pastry cutter, cut out 4 circles of bread. Place onto a baking tray covered with baking parchment, drizzle with a little rapeseed oil. Bake in the preheated oven for about 5 minutes, until crisp and golden brown.

To prepare the tartare, half an hour before serving, dice the scallops and strawberries into thumbnail-sized pieces; set aside the strawberries. Place the scallops into a bowl with the lime juice, olive oil, coriander and a good seasoning of salt and freshly ground black pepper. Mix well and set aside until needed.

To serve, add the strawberries and lime rind to the scallop tartare. Mix well, check the seasoning and serve a good portion of the tartare on each of the bread crisps.

Serves Four

for the crisps:
4 slices of bread
rapeseed oil

for the tartare:
4 king scallops,
cleaned, roe removed
4 large strawberries, *hulled*
juice and rind of half a lime
2 tbsp light olive oil
1 tbsp chopped coriander
sea salt & black pepper

SEA BASS/
TOMATO FEUILLETINE & NASTURTIUM PESTO

To make the pesto, place all the ingredients into a liquidiser and season with salt and freshly ground black pepper. Blitz really well, season again, and set aside.

To make the feuilletine, on a lightly floured surface roll out the pastry, straight from the fridge, as thinly as you can. Cut out 8 rectangular pieces of pastry about 10 x 6cms and place on a greaseproof-covered baking tray. Prick all over with a fork and rest in the fridge for 30 minutes.

Preheat the oven to 180°C/350°F/gas mark 4. Remove the pastry from the fridge and cover with greaseproof paper. Place a baking tray on top to weigh it down and prevent it from rising. Bake in the oven for 20 minutes; the pastry should be golden and crisp. Remove from the oven and leave uncovered on the baking tray.

Score the tops of the tomatoes with a knife and blanch them in a pan of boiling water for 30 seconds, then remove from the heat and remove the skins. Slice the tomatoes thinly and set aside.

To cook the sea bass, preheat the grill to high. Cut the sea bass into 8 even-sized fillets and place skin side up onto a lightly oiled baking tray. Using a blowtorch colour the skin slightly until darkened, brush with a little oil, season with salt and freshly ground black pepper. Place the sea bass under the preheated grill, skin side up, for 3 minutes – the flesh will just start to pull away when the fish is cooked.

To serve, reheat the pastry in the oven and place 2 pieces on each serving plate. Use 1 tomato per serving to cover the pastry, and season with salt and freshly ground black pepper. Cover the tomatoes with a fillet of sea bass and finish with a serving of nasturtium pesto.

Serves Four

for the pesto:
75g fresh nasturtium leaves
75g roasted pine kernels
100g Parmesan, *grated*
75g garlic-infused olive oil
sea salt & black pepper

for the feuilletine:
300g all-butter puff pastry
4 vine tomatoes

for the sea bass:
4 fillets of sea bass, *descaled, trimmed, pin bones removed*
olive oil
sea salt & black pepper

Quick and easy

BLOW-TORCHED SEA BREAM/ SAUTERNES & CURRY SAUCE

Serves Four

for the curry sauce:
55g salted butter
2 large shallots, *peeled, finely sliced*
150g button mushrooms, *finely sliced*
35g plain flour
1 tbsp mild curry powder
300ml Sauternes white wine
600ml white fish stock *see page 238*
150ml double cream
sea salt & black pepper

for the sea bream:
4 fillets of sea bream, *descaled, pin bones removed*
rapeseed oil
sea salt & black pepper

To make the curry sauce, melt the butter in a heavy-based saucepan, add the shallots and mushrooms, sauté until softened but not coloured. Add the flour and curry powder and continue to cook for a further 4 to 5 minutes, stirring continuously.

Pour in the Sauternes, scrape the pan well, turn up the heat a little and bubble to reduce by a third. Add the fish stock, bring to a gentle simmer and cook for roughly 30 minutes, whisking occasionally, until the sauce is thick enough to coat the back of a spoon – the sauce should cling to the spoon rather than run off. Add the cream, check the consistency again, season with salt and freshly ground pepper, and then pass through a sieve and set aside.

To grill the sea bream, preheat the grill to high. Place the fillets onto a baking tray skin side up, brush with rapeseed oil and season with salt and freshly ground black pepper.

Darken the skin slightly using a blowtorch, and place the baking tray under the grill for 5 minutes until the skin is crisp and the flesh is just starting to turn opaque.

Serve with a splash of the curry sauce.

SHRIMP & SPELT BATTER SCRAPS

To make the batter, place 150g of spelt flour into a bowl and season with salt and freshly ground black pepper. Slowly add in enough sparkling water to make a runny batter, with the consistency of thin cream, whisk until smooth and set aside.

To make the shrimp scraps, heat the oil in a deep fat fryer to 180°C. Lightly coat the shrimps in the remaining flour, and drop them into the batter. Remove from the batter using a slotted spoon and shake off any excess. Drop the coated shrimps into the fryer and fry briefly until they are crisp and golden brown. Remove from the fryer and drain well on kitchen paper.

Serve garnished with flakes of sea salt and a good squeeze of lime juice.

Serves Four

for the batter:
200g spelt flour
sea salt & black pepper
400ml sparkling water

for the shrimp scraps:
1 litre vegetable oil, *for frying*
250g brown shrimps, *peeled*
2 limes, *halved, lightly charred*
sea salt

Quick and easy

CRAB/SM

LOBS
MUS
PRAWNS
SMOKED SALM
SQ

*Appetisers, snacks & starters

SMALL PLATES*

OKED HADDOCK
LANGOU
TER/M
SELS/OYSTERS
IGER PRAWNS
ON/SARDINES
UID/WHITEBAIT

CANNELLONI OF CRAB & AVOCADO/ ROASTED TOMATOES

To roast the tomatoes, heat the oven to 100°C/210°F/gas mark ¼. Place the tomatoes onto a baking tray, season with salt and freshly ground black pepper and drizzle with a good helping of rapeseed oil. Place in the oven for 1¼ hours – the tomatoes will shrivel slightly and the flavour will intensify. Remove from the oven and set aside.

To make the cannelloni, pick over the crab meat making sure there is no shell in it, place into a bowl with the mayonnaise, chopped coriander and a good seasoning of salt and freshly ground black pepper. Spoon the mixture into a piping bag and refrigerate.

Peel the avocados, cut in half, remove the stone and then slice lengthways as thinly as possible. Lay out 4 pieces of cling film on your work surface and along the centre of each piece lay the slices from half an avocado to about 20cm in length, slightly overlapping each slice. Sprinkle with lemon juice and lightly season with sea salt.

Pipe the chilled crab meat just off centre along the length of the avocado slices and then using the cling film roll up tightly like a sausage and tie each end. Refrigerate to firm up for 1 hour.

Remove the cannelloni from the fridge, cut each one into 4 pieces and carefully remove the cling film.

Serve with the roasted tomatoes and elderflower mayonnaise, and garnish with flakes of sea salt.

Serves Four

for the roasted tomatoes:
12 cherry tomatoes, *sliced in half*
sea salt & black pepper
rapeseed oil

for the cannelloni:
200g fresh white crab meat
1 tbsp mayonnaise
2 tbsp chopped coriander
sea salt & black pepper
2 ripe avocados
lemon juice
elderflower mayonnaise,
see page 71

Small plates

CRAB BON BONS/ ELDERFLOWER MAYONNAISE

To make the crab bon bons, pick over the crab meat to ensure there is no shell in it and place into a bowl together with the egg yolk and sieved mashed potato. Season well with salt and freshly ground pepper, and combine the mixture with your hands. Make a small ball of the mixture (about the size of a quail's egg) and place onto a tray covered with greaseproof paper. Repeat with the remaining mixture.

Place the plain flour, whisked egg wash and Panko breadcrumbs into three separate bowls. Take one of the crab balls and coat lightly with flour, then dip it into the egg wash, shaking off any excess before finally dipping it into the breadcrumbs and covering well. Place the bon bons onto another greaseproof-covered tray. Repeat the process until all the crab balls are floured, egg-washed and coated in breadcrumbs. Chill them in the fridge until needed.

Serves Four

for the crab bon bons:
250g white crab meat
1 egg yolk
100g mashed potato,
passed through a sieve
sea salt & black pepper
100g seasoned plain flour
1 egg and 150ml milk,
whisked together
150g Panko breadcrumbs
1 litre vegetable oil, *for frying*

for the mayonnaise:
1 egg
1 tbsp white wine vinegar
2 tbsp lemon juice
2 tsp Dijon mustard,
or 1 tsp English mustard powder
sea salt & black pepper
300ml grapeseed oil
2 tbsp elderflower cordial

To make the mayonnaise, place the egg, vinegar and lemon juice into the bowl of a food processor with the mustard and a good seasoning of salt and freshly ground black pepper. Whizz on a high speed and then very slowly drizzle in the grapeseed oil (the mixture will emulsify and thicken). At the end, add the elderflower cordial and check the seasoning. Chill in the fridge until needed.

To serve, heat the oil in a deep-sided pan to 180°C. Carefully drop in the chilled bon bons, and fry for 1 minute. Remove from the hot oil using a slotted spoon, and drain on kitchen paper. Serve hot with the mayonnaise.

CRAB CAKES/ PICKLED SAMPHIRE

To pickle the samphire, bring a pan of unsalted water to the boil, drop in the samphire and blanch for a couple of minutes. Refresh under cold running water, drain thoroughly and pat dry on kitchen paper. Place the vinegar and sugar into a saucepan and over a low heat allow the sugar to dissolve. Turn up the heat and bring to the boil, add the chilli, herbs, coriander seeds and white peppercorns. Remove from the heat and leave to infuse and cool. Transfer the samphire to the pickling liquor, season well with salt and freshly ground pepper, and store in a container in the fridge. The pickled samphire is ready to eat after 1 hour, but will keep for up to a month.

To make the crab cakes, using your fingers flake the white crab meat into a bowl making sure there are no bits of shell. Combine the meat with the beaten egg yolks and coriander. Season with salt and freshly ground black pepper. Divide the mixture into 4 and, using your hands, form into even-sized cakes, place on a tray and put in the freezer for 30 minutes to firm the mixture up.

Put the seasoned flour, whisked egg wash and breadcrumbs into three separate bowls. Remove the crab cakes from the freezer. Dip each cake into the seasoned flour, then into the egg wash, shaking off any excess as you go. Finally, dip each one into the breadcrumbs, making sure they are lightly and evenly coated. Place the finished crab cakes on a tray lined with greaseproof paper, cover with cling film and refrigerate until ready to use.

Heat a large heavy-based frying pan over a medium heat. Once hot, add a splash of olive oil together with the butter. Fry the crab cakes gently for about 4 minutes on each side until they are crisp and lightly golden.

Serve hot with the pickled samphire.

Serves Four

for the pickled samphire:
200g samphire, *carefully picked over, washed thoroughly*
250g cider vinegar
250g caster sugar
1 large red chilli, *finely sliced*
2 bay leaves
1 sprig tarragon
1 sprig thyme
1 tsp coriander seeds
½ tsp white peppercorns
sea salt & black pepper

for the crab cakes:
250g white crab meat
2 egg yolks, *beaten*
4 tbsp chopped coriander
sea salt & black pepper
100g seasoned plain flour
1 egg and 100ml milk, *whisked together*
175g white breadcrumbs
olive oil
1 knob of salted butter

Small plates

Small plates

CRAB JELLY/
PEA PANNA COTTA

To make the panna cotta, place the gelatine leaves into a tray of cold water to soak. Heat the cream and milk in a saucepan over a medium heat, bring to the boil and remove from the heat. Lift the soaked gelatine leaves from the water, squeezing out any excess water with your hands, and stir into the hot cream to dissolve thoroughly. Place the milk and cream, petits pois, sugar and a few mint leaves into a liquidiser, season well with salt and freshly ground black pepper and blitz thoroughly. Pass through a sieve and pour into suitable glasses or individual ramekins. Refrigerate to firm up for 2 hours.

To make the crab jelly, heat the apple juice with 150ml water in a saucepan together with the mint, tarragon and lemon juice until boiling. Remove from the heat and set aside to infuse for 30 minutes, then pass through a sieve.

Place the gelatine leaves into a tray of cold water to soak. Reheat the apple stock in a saucepan. Remove the gelatine from the water, squeezing out any excess with your hands, and then stir it into the warmed stock to dissolve thoroughly. Refrigerate it to firm up for 1 hour.

Pick over the crab meat to ensure there is no shell in it and season well with salt and freshly ground black pepper. Fry the spring onions in a little rapeseed oil until softened, but not coloured, drain on kitchen paper and set aside.

Just before the jelly has set, stir in the crab meat and cooled spring onions. Spread the jelly over the top of the set pea panna cotta. Refrigerate it again to firm up for another 2 hours (it can be chilled for up to 12 hours).

Serve once firm and chilled.

Serves Four

for the panna cotta:
6 leaves of gelatine
180ml double cream
50ml full fat milk
350g petits pois, *blanched, refreshed*
45g sugar
2 large sprigs of fresh mint
sea salt & black pepper

for the crab jelly:
250ml clear apple juice
1 sprig of mint
1 large sprig of tarragon
juice of half a lemon
8 leaves of gelatine
200g white crab meat
6 spring onions, *finely sliced*
rapeseed oil
sea salt & black pepper

CRAB TOASTIES/ POTATO- WRAPPED QUAILS' EGGS

Serves Four

for the potato-wrapped eggs:
8 quails' eggs
1 large Maris Piper potato, *peeled*
1 litre vegetable oil, *for frying*
sea salt & black pepper

for the toasties:
100g white crab meat
50g cream cheese
2 tbsp mayonnaise
15g breadcrumbs
1 tsp soy sauce
1 pinch of cayenne pepper
sea salt & black pepper
1 small loaf sourdough bread,
thinly sliced diagonally

To make the potato-wrapped eggs, bring a small pan of lightly salted water to the boil. Lower in the eggs and boil for 2 minutes 30 seconds. Remove from the pan and refresh immediately under cold running water. When cold, peel the eggs and set aside in a bowl of cold water.

Bring another pan of salted water to the boil. Using a spiraliser make long strands of potato string out of the potato. Drop the potato strings into the boiling water and blanch for 2 minutes. Refresh immediately under cold running water and drain thoroughly. Lay out on kitchen paper and pat dry.

To make the toasties, preheat the oven to 180°C/350°F/gas mark 4. Pick over the crab meat and remove any small pieces of shell. Soften the cream cheese at room temperature, then mix together with the mayonnaise and crab meat. Add the breadcrumbs and soy sauce and season with cayenne pepper, salt and freshly ground black pepper. Lightly toast 4 slices of sourdough bread, then spread the crab mix evenly on the bread. Place on a baking tray, and bake in the oven for 10 minutes.

While the toasties are in the oven, heat the oil in a deep fat fryer to 180°C. Wrap the potato strings around the quails' eggs, so that they are totally covered, then lower them into the fryer. Fry for 2 minutes until the potato is crisp and golden all over. Remove from the fryer, and drain on kitchen paper. Season with salt and freshly ground black pepper.

Serve the crab toasties straight from the oven with the potato-wrapped eggs.

Small plates

SMOKED HADDOCK SCOTCH QUAILS' EGGS/ LIME MAYONNAISE

Serves Four

for the mayonnaise:
juice of 2 limes, *plus zest of 1 lime*
1 tbsp white wine vinegar
1 egg
1 tsp English mustard powder
275ml sunflower oil
sea salt & black pepper

for the mousse:
275g smoked haddock
100ml double cream
juice of 1 lemon

for the Scotch eggs:
12 quails' eggs, *3 per serving*
1 medium egg yolk, *beaten*
100g seasoned plain flour
75g Panko breadcrumbs,
or stale bread left out overnight so it blitzes well for breadcrumbs
1 litre vegetable oil, *for frying*
sea salt & black pepper

To make the mayonnaise, place 2 tablespoons of the lime juice into the bowl of a food processor with the white wine vinegar, egg and mustard powder. Season well with salt and freshly ground pepper, then whizz on a high speed until all the ingredients are combined. Slowly drizzle in the sunflower oil with the processor still running; the mixture will emulsify and gradually thicken. Add the lime zest and more lime juice if necessary. Check the seasoning and refrigerate until ready to use.

To make the mousse, mince the smoked haddock, place in a bowl with the cream and lemon juice and combine well. Cover and refrigerate for 1 hour to firm up.

To make the Scotch eggs, bring a small pan of lightly salted water to the boil. Lower in the eggs and boil for 2 minutes 30 seconds. Remove from the pan and refresh immediately under cold running water. When cold, peel the eggs and set aside in a bowl of cold water.

Use three separate bowls: place the seasoned flour into one, the beaten egg into another, and place the breadcrumbs into the third.

Drain the eggs and dry pat dry with kitchen paper. Working quickly, take a portion of the mousse and flatten it in the palm of your hand. Place an egg in the centre and wrap the mousse around the egg so that it's totally encased. Gently shape the mousse evenly around the egg, moulding it with your hands, and repeat with the other eggs.

Roll each wrapped egg in seasoned flour, then dip into the beaten egg, shaking off any excess. Finally, roll them in the breadcrumbs to coat thoroughly and place on to a baking tray covered with greaseproof paper.

Heat the oil in a deep fat fryer to 180°C. Lower the eggs into the hot oil and fry until lightly coloured and crisp all over. You may need to do this in batches: if so, make sure the oil comes back up to 180°C before frying the next batch. Remove the cooked eggs with a slotted spoon and drain on kitchen paper.

Serve hot, with the lime mayonnaise on the side.

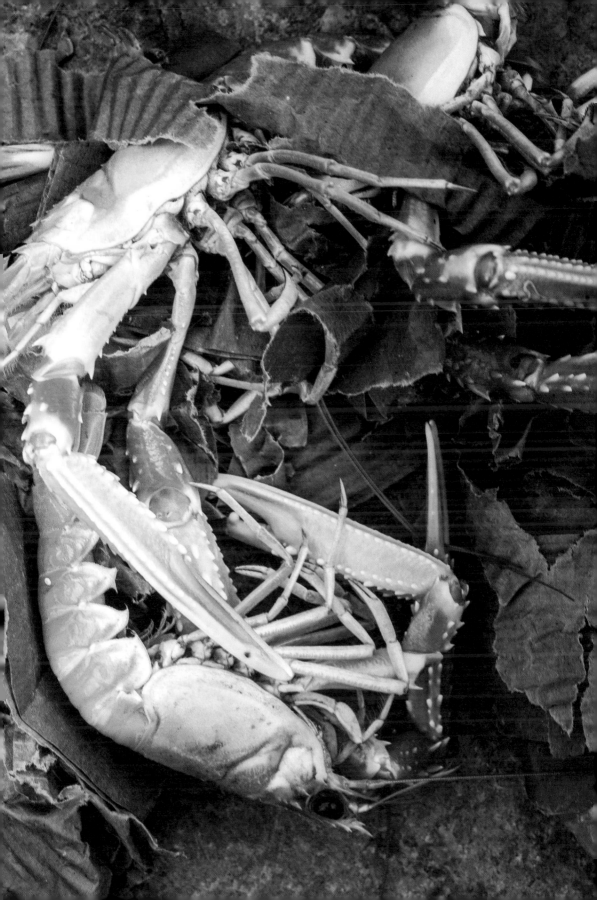

"THE TRICK TO BUYING
IT SIMPLE. I'M LUCKY
THE SEA AND HAVE DI
WITH GREAT FISHERM
SUPPLIERS OVER THE
RESEARCH AND TAKE
THE RIGHT SUPPLIER V

SEAFOOD IS KEEPING
ENOUGH TO LIVE BY
/ELOPED RELATIONSHIPS
=N AND SEAFOOD
YEARS. DO YOUR
YOUR TIME TO FIND
HO YOU CAN TRUST"

LANGOUSTINES/
PEANUT SAUCE

Live langoustines are a rare treat and need to be treated with care and admiration. This is a truly delicious way of enjoying them.

To make the peanut sauce, heat a pan over a moderate heat, add the rapeseed oil and butter followed by the shallots, garlic, chilli, ginger and lemongrass and sweat until lightly caramelised. Add the shrimp paste, tomatoes and sugar, continue to sauté and allow to catch very slightly. Next add the langoustine stock and scrape the pan well to deglaze. Turn up the heat a little and simmer to reduce by half. Add the coconut milk and continue to boil to reduce by half again. Pass the sauce through a fine sieve into a food processor together with the roasted peanuts, blitz thoroughly and set aside.

To prepare the langoustines, remove the heads and then pull the bottom of the tails to remove the black spinal trail. Bring a pan of water to the boil, drop in the langoustines and blanch for 10 seconds. Refresh immediately under cold running water and drain thoroughly. Peel off the outer shells, cover and set aside.

Add the vegetable oil to a small saucepan until it's one third full, and heat to 190°C. Add the wild rice and it will immediately puff up; take out with a slotted spoon and drain on kitchen paper. Season with sea salt, freshly ground black pepper, a splash of vinegar and a good pinch of sugar, and set aside.

Heat a pan over a medium heat, add a knob of butter and gently pan-fry the langoustines to heat right through and lightly colour.

Reheat the peanut sauce and check the seasoning (if there's any leftover sauce after serving it can be frozen).

To serve, drizzle some peanut sauce onto each plate and place the langoustines on top, garnish with puffed wild rice and micro coriander.

Serves Four

for the peanut sauce:
50ml rapeseed oil
25g salted butter
10 shallots, *peeled, finely sliced*
10 garlic cloves, *peeled, grated*
1 red chilli, *deseeded, finely sliced*
50g fresh ginger, *peeled, grated*
5 stalks lemongrass, *crushed*
100g shrimp paste
600g tomatoes, *roughly chopped*
200g muscovado sugar
500ml langoustine stock,
see page 240
250g coconut milk
250g roasted salted peanuts

for the langoustines:
24 large langoustines, *6 per serving*
1 litre vegetable oil, *for frying*
100g wild rice, *puffed*
sea salt & black pepper
1 tbsp white wine vinegar
1 tbsp sugar
1 knob of salted butter
1 handful of micro coriander leaves

Small plates

BLACK LOBSTER TEMPURA/ THAI GREEN EMULSION

Serves Four

for the emulsion:

6 tbsp fresh coriander
6 tbsp fresh mint leaves
4 Kaffir lime leaves
zest of 1 lemon
4 sticks lemongrass,
crushed, chopped
1 tbsp fresh ginger, *grated*
1 green chilli, *finely sliced*
15g galangal
400ml sunflower oil
1 egg
1 tbsp lemon juice
1 tbsp white wine vinegar
2 tsp Dijon mustard,
or 1 tsp English mustard powder
sea salt & black pepper

for the lobster tempura:

200g gluten-free self-raising flour
½ tsp sea salt
1 tsp squid ink
400ml sparkling water
1 litre vegetable oil, *for frying*
2 lobsters,
meat cut into large nuggets
100g seasoned plain flour

To make the emulsion, bring a pan of water to the boil, drop in the coriander and mint leaves, blanch for 2 minutes and immediately refresh under cold running water. Drain thoroughly and pat dry on kitchen paper.

Place the Kaffir leaves, lemon zest, lemongrass, grated ginger, chilli, galangal and 100ml sunflower oil into a saucepan and gently heat through. Transfer to a liquidiser together with the coriander and mint and blitz thoroughly. Pass through a fine sieve and set aside to cool.

Place the egg, lemon juice and white wine vinegar into the bowl of a food processor with the mustard and a good seasoning of salt and freshly ground black pepper. Whizz on a high speed and very slowly drizzle in the remaining 300ml of sunflower oil. The mixture will emulsify and then thicken. Remove from the food processor and fold in the cooled liquid, check the seasoning and set aside.

To make the lobster tempura, place the gluten-free self-raising flour (gluten-free flour produces a very light batter) into a bowl with the salt and squid ink, and add enough sparkling mineral water to make a runny, lumpy batter, with the consistency of thin cream. Set aside.

Add the vegetable oil to a heavy-based pan until it's one third full, and heat up to 180°C.

Dust the lobster nuggets in the seasoned flour then, using a fork or wooden skewer, dip them into the batter, then drop into the heated oil. Fry for about 2 minutes and then remove from the oil and drain on kitchen paper.

Serve with the Thai green emulsion.

MACKEREL TART/ BEETROOT & FENNEL SALAD

Serves Four

for the mackerel tart:
75g rock salt
4 mackerel fillets,
prepared with all bones removed
200g rice wine vinegar
3 tbsp sugar
juice of 1 lemon
1 tbsp cumin seeds
200g all-butter puff pastry
60g salted butter
4 shallots, *peeled, finely sliced*

for the salad:
1 large golden beetroot
1 bulb fennel
1 orange
4 baby cooked beetroots
champagne vinegar
olive oil
sea salt & black pepper

To make the mackerel tart, spread half of the rock salt onto a tray just large enough to hold the mackerel. Place the fillets on top and cover with the remaining salt. Make sure the fish is evenly coated with the salt, and set it aside for 2 hours. Then rinse the fillets under cold running water and set aside.

Mix 200g of water with the rice wine vinegar, sugar, lemon juice and cumin seeds together in a deep-sided tray. Place the fish into the liquid for 2 hours, then remove the fish and set aside.

Preheat the oven to 190°C/375°F/gas mark 5. Roll out the puff pastry to about 0.5cm thick and place on a baking tray lined with greaseproof paper. Place another piece of greaseproof paper over the pastry and another baking tray on top of it. Bake in the preheated oven for about 20 minutes until the pastry is golden brown. Remove from the oven and cool.

At the same time heat a frying pan over a medium heat, add the butter and sweat the shallots very slowly until soft and translucent. Remove from the pan and allow to cool.

Preheat the oven to 180°C/350°F/gas mark 4. Very carefully cut the cooked puff pastry into 4 pieces the same size as the mackerel fillets.

Slice the mackerel fillets as thinly as possible, retaining the shape of the fillet.

Divide the softened shallot into 4 and spread over the pastry, then carefully place the finely sliced mackerel on top. Place in the preheated oven to heat through for 2 minutes.

To prepare the salad, slice the golden beetroot and fennel very thinly (retain the fronds of the fennel for garnish) and place into a bowl. Peel and segment the orange and add to the bowl with the cooked beetroot.

Dress 4 salads with a little champagne vinegar, olive oil, salt and freshly ground black pepper. Garnish with the fennel fronds, and serve each with a hot mackerel tart.

MUSSEL GRATIN

Serves Four

for the purée:
900g shallots, *ends trimmed*
120ml olive oil
1 fresh thyme sprig
sea salt & black pepper
1 knob of salted butter
150ml double cream

for the mussels:
2kg mussels
50g salted butter
200g shallots, *peeled, finely sliced*
1 garlic clove, *peeled, finely sliced*
1 sprig of thyme
200ml dry white wine
1 handful sea vegetables,
*such as sea asters, sea beets,
samphire, sea purslane*

for the crumb topping:
100g ground almonds
100g Parmesan, *grated*
50g Panko breadcrumbs
1 tbsp chopped parsley
sea salt & black pepper

To make the purée, preheat the oven to 180°C/350°F/gas mark 4. Lay 2 large sheets of foil on top of each other on a work surface. Place the shallots in the centre of the foil, pour over the olive oil, add the thyme and season well with salt and freshly ground black pepper. Draw the sides of the foil up to the centre and crinkle the edges to seal and form a parcel. Place on a baking tray and roast in the oven for 1½ hours until the shallots are really soft.

Remove the papery shallot skins and place the shallots in a liquidiser with the butter and cream. Blitz really well and pour into a bowl. Check the seasoning and set aside.

To prepare the mussels, clean and scrub the mussels under cold running water, making sure all the beards are removed, and set aside.

Heat a large deep-sided pan over a moderate heat, add the butter, shallots, garlic and thyme and sweat off until the onions are softened but not coloured. Turn the heat up high, throw in the mussels and add the wine. Cover the pan and steam for 2 minutes. Once the mussels have opened, drain well, retaining the cooking liquor and discarding any mussels which have not opened. Pass the cooking liquor through a muslin-lined sieve and retain.

Pick the mussels from their shells and cover. Retain the larger halves of the shells for serving.

To make the crumb topping, combine all the ingredients in a bowl, season well with salt and freshly ground pepper, and set aside.

To serve, preheat the grill to high. Spoon the purée into the mussel shells and place a mussel on top. Spoon over some of the cooking liquor and cover with crumb topping. Place under the preheated grill for 2 to 3 minutes; the topping should be well coloured.

Serve hot on a bed of sea vegetables.

OYSTER CRACKERS

This is a complex recipe which at first appears a bit daunting but is well worth the effort for the stunning results. The crackers freeze well, and go well with the oyster tartare on page 48.

The recipe doesn't scale down: to get 400g of oyster juice you will need the juice from roughly 40 oysters, but only need the flesh from 6, you'll also need a Thermomix and a vac pack machine. You can use the remaining 34 oysters for other recipes, on pages 48 and 167.

Shuck all of the oysters, retaining as much juice as possible; you'll need roughly 400g oyster juice. Strain the juice through a muslin cloth.

Place 6 oysters, the flour, chicken stock and the oyster juice into a Thermomix and blend on full power at 90°C for 15 minutes.

Once cooked, spread the mixture on a tray lined with a non-stick mat. Place in a dehydrator at 55°C for 12 hours to dehydrate. If you don't have a dehydrator then place in an oven set at the lowest temperature until completely dry; this will probably take 8 to 12 hours.

Once dry, break into shards, seal in the vac pac machine and store in the freezer until needed.

Serves Four

40 whole oysters
200g tapioca flour
200ml chicken stock, *see page 236*
1 litre vegetable oil, *for frying*
1 handful of oyster leaves, *optional*

To serve, heat the oil in a deep fat fryer to 220°C. Drop the oyster shards into the oil and fry for a few seconds: they will puff up immediately.

Remove from the fryer, drain on kitchen paper and serve with a handful of oyster leaves.

PRAWN & CRAB SUMMER ROLLS/ VIETNAMESE DIPPING SAUCE

Serves Four

for the dipping sauce:

2 tbsp white wine vinegar
4 tbsp lime juice
1 chilli, *deseeded, finely sliced*
3 garlic cloves, *peeled, grated*
1 small lobe of ginger,
peeled, grated
8 tbsp nam pla fish sauce
4 tbsp caster sugar

for the summer rolls:

½ small white cabbage,
core removed, very finely sliced
2 carrots, *peeled,*
cut into fine julienne strips
2 red onions, *peeled,*
core removed, very finely sliced
1 handful of fresh mint, *chopped*
2 handfuls of fresh coriander
100g beansprouts
2 dressed crabs
36 cooked tiger prawns, *shelled*
12 x 22cm round rice
paper wrappers

To make the dipping sauce, whisk all the ingredients together with 250ml of water in a bowl, and refrigerate until ready to use.

To make the summer rolls, place the cabbage, carrots and onions into a large bowl together with the mint, chopped coriander and beansprouts and mix well so that all the ingredients are evenly distributed; set aside.

Pick the crab meat out of the shell, making sure there are no bits of shell left in it. Gently mix the white and brown meat together in a bowl being careful not to break it up too much; set aside.

Set out all the components of the dish within easy reach of a clean dry chopping board.

Half fill a bowl large enough to fit the rice papers in with cold water. Dunk each one into the water for 25 to 30 seconds until pliable, lay on the chopping board and pat dry.

Arrange 3 prawns along the bottom edge of the rice paper and sprinkle with the crab meat, then arrange the vegetable mixture on top of the crab and prawns.

Bring the bottom of the wrapper tightly up and over the filling and then fold the sides in and over. Continue to roll up tightly until it resembles a spring roll shape and set aside. Repeat until all the mixture and prawns are used up.

Serve, dipping your summer roll into the dipping sauce with every bite.

TIGER PRAWN & CRAB WONTONS/ SALAD CREAM

To make the salad cream, whisk the mustard, sugar, vinegar and salt together in a bowl, then whisk in the evaporated milk. Gradually whisk in the oil to emulsify. Refrigerate until ready to use.

Serves Four

for the salad cream:
1 tsp English mustard
1 tsp caster sugar
3 tbsp white wine vinegar
$\frac{1}{2}$ tsp sea salt
150ml evaporated milk
150ml vegetable oil

for the wontons:
200g fresh white crab meat
6 raw tiger prawns, *peeled, deveined*
1 red chilli, *deseeded, finely sliced*
1 small lobe of ginger, *peeled, grated*
2 garlic cloves, *peeled, grated*
1 handful of coriander, *chopped*
1 packet of wonton wraps
1 egg beaten, *for egg wash*
1 litre vegetable oil, *for frying*
2 tbsp sesame seeds

To make the wontons, place the crab meat into a bowl, chop the tiger prawns roughly and add to the crab meat with the chopped chilli. Add the ginger and garlic to the bowl and throw in the chopped coriander and mix well.

Place a wonton wrapper on a work surface and add 1 teaspoon of the mixture in the centre. Brush all four edges of the wrapper with the egg wash, fold the wonton in half (corner to corner) to make a triangle and seal tightly, making sure there are no air pockets or holes. Fold the longer two triangle points together to make the wonton shape and set aside – repeat until the mixture is used up.

Heat the oil in a deep fat fryer to 180°C. Deep fry the wontons until golden brown in colour.

Remove from the fryer, drain on kitchen paper and serve hot garnished with sesame seeds, and with the salad cream.

TIGER PRAWN & HARICOT BEAN SOUP/ CURRY OIL

Serves Four

for the curry oil:
300ml rapeseed oil
2 tbsp medium curry powder
1 garlic clove, *peeled, smashed*
1/2 tsp ground turmeric
1/2 tsp fennel seeds
1 pinch smoked cayenne pepper

for the soup:
250g dried haricot beans,
soaked overnight in cold water
1 small onion, *peeled, halved*
1 carrot, *peeled, sliced*
1 bouquet garni, *thyme,*
bay leaf and parsley tied together
300ml chicken stock
150ml double cream
sea salt & black pepper
30g cold salted butter, *cut into*
cubes, plus a few knobs for frying
12 tiger prawns, *peeled, deveined, left*
whole or cut into bite-sized pieces

To make the curry oil, place the ingredients into a saucepan over a very low heat and simmer for 30 minutes. Remove from the heat and allow to cool before straining the oil through a very fine sieve. Set aside until needed.

To make the soup, drain the haricot beans and place in a saucepan. Add the onion, carrot and bouquet garni and cover with cold water. Bring to the boil and boil steadily for 10 minutes, then lower the heat to a simmer. Cover the pan and cook for 45 minutes until the beans are soft, stirring occasionally.

Drain the beans and discard the onions, carrot and bouquet garni. Place the beans into a clean pan, add the stock and cream and bring to the boil over a medium heat. Transfer to a blender and blitz. Sieve the soup into a pan, season with salt and freshly ground pepper, stir in the butter and keep it warm until needed.

In a large frying pan over a medium heat, add a knob or two of butter and sauté the prawns until just cooked.

To serve, pour the warm soup into bowls, pile the cooked prawns into the centre and drizzle with a little curry oil.

SMOKED SALMON/ NASTURTIUM PESTO & PRESSED POTATOES

Serves Four

for the pesto:
75g fresh nasturtium leaves
75g roasted pine kernels
100g Parmesan, *grated*
75g garlic-infused olive oil
sea salt & black pepper

for the pressed potatoes:
10 large Maris Piper potatoes
200ml melted butter
12 sprigs of fresh thyme,
leaves stripped from the stalk
sea salt & black pepper
rapeseed oil

for the salmon:
450g smoked salmon fillet,
cut into 1-2cm steaks
1 handful of nasturtium leaves

To make the pesto, place all the ingredients into a liquidiser and season with salt and freshly ground black pepper. Blitz really well, check the seasoning and refrigerate until ready to use.

To make the pressed potatoes, preheat the oven to 160°C/325°F/gas mark 3. Peel the potatoes and slice really thinly (this is best done using a mandoline).

Cover the base of a well-buttered ovenproof dish, approximately 30 x 22cms, with rows of sliced potatoes overlapping slightly. Do the same with another layer of potatoes but in the opposite direction. Do a third layer in the same direction as the first layer. Drizzle over some melted butter, scatter over some thyme leaves and season well with salt and freshly ground black pepper.

Repeat this process until you have filled the dish, drizzling over melted butter, scattering thyme and seasoning on each third layer of potatoes. Cover with greaseproof paper and foil. Place the dish in the centre of the preheated oven and cook for 1½ hours; test to see if the potatoes are cooked by inserting a skewer, if it slides in easily, the potatoes are done.

Remove from the oven and place an even weight on top of the potatoes to firm. When cool place in the fridge (still with the weight on) overnight.

Remove the potatoes from the fridge and remove the foil and greaseproof paper. Turn the dish upside down on a work surface and use a blowtorch to gently warm the bottom and side of the dish to allow the potatoes to slip out. Use a sharp knife to cut into 1-2cm portions.

Finally, heat a frying pan, add a good splash of rapeseed oil and pan fry the potatoes, turning regularly, to colour on both sides. Remove from the heat and keep them warm.

To sear the salmon, heat a heavy-based ridged frying pan until nearly smoking, place the salmon steaks across the ridges of the pan and press down for 30 seconds, then turn the steaks over and repeat on the other side.

Serve the salmon with the pressed potatoes, drizzle with pesto, and garnish with a few nasturtium leaves.

GRILLED SARDINES/ SEAWEED GREMOLATA

To make the gremolata, bring a pan of water to the boil, drop in the sea vegetables, chives, parsley and chervil, and blanch for 30 seconds. Drain and refresh in iced water, squeeze out as much moisture as possible and place in a food processor together with all the remaining ingredients and season well with salt and freshly ground black pepper. Pulse in the food processor – you're not looking for a very smooth liquid, more of a rough rustic texture.

Serves Four

12 sardines, *prepared and filleted*

for the gremolata:
100g sea vegetables, *such as sea beets, sea asters, samphire*
25g chives
50g parsley
30g chervil
200g good quality olive oil
2 garlic cloves, *peeled, grated*
1 red chilli, *deseeded, finely sliced*
grated zest from 1 lemon
sea salt & black pepper

To grill the sardines, preheat the grill to high when ready to serve. Place the sardines skin side up on a grill tray, baste generously with gremolata and place under the grill for 3 minutes. The best way to check if the sardines are cooked is with a cocktail stick – if it slips through the centre of the fish, then they're cooked.

Serve hot with some crusty sourdough bread, good quality salted butter and maybe a lightly dressed watercress salad.

SALT & PEPPER SQUID

A favourite of mine and a classic, which is 100% reliant on wonderful fresh squid.

Serves Four

for the flour:
250g cornflour
250g rice flour
2 tsp five spice powder
4 tsp crushed black pepper
2 tsp sea salt
3 tsp Szechuan pepper
2 tsp ground ginger

for the squid:
400g fresh baby squid
4 egg whites
1 litre vegetable oil, *for frying*
the zest of 1 lime
sea salt
2 limes, *cut into wedges*

To make the flour mixture, combine all of the ingredients together in a large bowl, making sure the spices are evenly distributed.

To cook the squid, strip the tentacles from the tubes and slice the tubes into rounds. Pat all the squid dry with kitchen paper and set aside.

In a bowl whisk the egg whites into stiff peaks, add the squid and coat them all over with the whisked egg whites.

Heat the oil in a deep fat fryer to 180°C. Lift the squid out of the egg whites and place into the flour mixture. Turn to coat well and shake off any excess flour. Fry in the deep fat fryer until golden brown and crispy.

Serve scattered with lime zest and flakes of sea salt with a good squeeze of lime juice.

Small plates

SQUID INK CRACKERS WITH SMOKED SALMON/ LEMON PUREE

Serves Four

for the purée:
3 lemons
400g sugar

for the crackers:
400g fresh squid
14g salt
360g tapioca starch
40g squid ink
1 litre vegetable oil, *for frying*
250g smoked salmon, *thinly sliced*
50g mixed sea vegetables,
such as sandwort, sea beets,
samphire, sea purslane

This recipe isn't one for the faint-hearted! The crackers are stunning but involve a lot of preparation, but once made they will keep for several weeks in an airtight container.

To make the purée, prick the lemons fairly deeply all over and place into a saucepan with cold water to cover. Bring to the boil then remove from the heat and repeat this twice more, using fresh water each time.

In a separate pan bring 400ml water and the sugar to the boil and simmer for 15 minutes to make a syrup.

Place the lemons into a clean saucepan and cover with syrup, bring to the boil, simmer and cook until the lemons are very soft. Remove from the heat and allow to cool in the syrup. Put the lemons with 275ml of the syrup and blitz in a liquidiser for 10 minutes. Pass through a fine sieve, and refrigerate until ready to use.

To make the crackers, purée the squid in a food processor, pass through a fine sieve, then return to the food processor with all the salt, tapioca and squid ink. Blitz well.

Divide the mixture into 10 large vacuum pack bags, roll the mixture out thinly in the bags and seal. Fill a deep-sided roasting tray with hot water and on top of the stove bring the water up to 100°C. Place the vacuum pack bags into the water for 45 minutes. Remove from the water, allow to cool, and then refrigerate to chill. Once chilled remove from the bag and cut the crackers into roughly rectangular pieces approximately 10 x 5cm in size.

Preheat the oven to 60°C/140°F/gas mark ¼, or as low as possible. Place the crackers onto a cooling rack and into the oven to dry out for up to 24 hours. At this stage the crackers can be kept in an airtight container for several weeks.

To serve, heat the oil in a deep-fat fryer to 190°C, drop in the crackers and they'll puff up extraordinarily. Lift them out of the oil with a slotted spoon and drain on kitchen paper.

Serve the squid ink crackers cold with thin slices of smoked salmon, lemon purée and garnish with a couple of sprigs of sea vegetables.

LAGER, SOY & GINGER-FRIED WHITEBAIT/ WASABI AÏOLI

Serves Four

for the aïoli:
1 tbsp of wasabi paste
1 tbsp white wine vinegar
juice of half a lemon
2 egg yolks
2 garlic cloves, *peeled, grated*
200ml light olive oil
sea salt & black pepper

for the marinade:
1 red chilli, *sliced into rings*
1 shallot, *grated*
4 garlic cloves, *peeled, grated*
1 large lobe of ginger, *peeled, grated*
250ml of lager
8 tbsp soy sauce
juice and grated zest of 4 limes
6 tbsp caster sugar
1 tbsp sesame oil
1 handful of chopped coriander

for the whitebait:
500g fresh whitebait
1 litre vegetable oil, *for frying*
100g seasoned flour
1 large red chilli, *sliced*
6 spring onions, *sliced*
3 tbsp chopped coriander
2 limes, *cut into wedges*

To make the aïoli, put the wasabi paste, vinegar, lemon juice, egg yolks and grated garlic into the bowl of a food processor. Whizz well and then slowly add in the olive oil to form an emulsion. Taste, season well with salt and freshly ground black pepper and set aside.

To marinate the whitebait, mix all the ingredients together in a bowl. Add the whitebait and cover. Leave to marinate for at least 2 hours.

To fry the whitebait, heat the oil in a deep fat fryer to 180°C. Remove the whitebait, along with the pieces of chilli, shallot, garlic, ginger and coriander, out from the marinade.

Coat the whitebait and pieces of chilli etc. in the seasoned flour and shake off the excess. Deep fry everything until brown and crisp. Lift out of the oil with a slotted spoon and drain on kitchen paper.

Serve the whitebait with slices of chilli, spring onions, coriander and freshly squeezed lime over the top, and dunk into the wasabi aïoli.

CRAB/BR
HAKE/LEMON
MUS
SCALL

SHR

*Food to keep you calm

STRESS
-FREE*

Stress-free

CRAB CHOWDER

Separate the crab meat, picking it over carefully to ensure there is no shell in it. Place the white and brown crab meat into separate bowls and set aside. Retain the crab shells.

Heat the olive oil in a large saucepan and fry the vegetables with the garlic until lightly coloured. Add the herb stalks, lemongrass, peppercorns, star anise and coriander seeds, then stir in the tomato purée and cook for 3 to 4 minutes.

Add the brandy and flambé. When the flame dies down, add the wine and let bubble until reduced to a sticky consistency. Pour in the chicken stock and add the brown crab meat together with the crab shells. Bring to a simmer and cook gently for 30 minutes.

Pass the stock through a fine sieve into a clean saucepan, pressing the residue in the sieve with the back of a ladle to extract as much liquid and flavour as possible. Place back onto the heat, bring to the boil and reduce by half to intensify the flavour, tasting as you do so. Whisk in the cream and bring back to a simmer to reduce a little to achieve a good soupy consistency. Whisk in the butter, a little at a time. Finally, season with salt and freshly ground black pepper and add a squeeze of lemon juice.

To serve, place the white crab meat into the bottom of 4 bowls and cover with the chowder. Enjoy with crusty wholemeal bread and the obligatory glass of chilled white wine.

Serves Four

4 large dressed crabs
2 tbsp olive oil
1 onion, *peeled, diced*
1 large carrot, *peeled, diced*
1 leek, *trimmed, sliced thinly*
1 celery stick, *trimmed, chopped*
4 garlic cloves, *peeled*
1 small handful of herb stalks,
basil, coriander, tarragon
2 lemongrass stalks,
cut in half lengthways
6 white peppercorns
3 star anise
10 coriander seeds
2 tbsp tomato purée
175ml brandy
300ml white wine
750ml chicken stock, *see page 236*
150 ml double cream
50g unsalted butter,
chopped in pieces
sea salt & black pepper
1 squeeze of lemon juice

CRAB & POTATO 'RISOTTO'

Place the whipping cream into a saucepan and bring to the boil; turn down the heat and simmer to reduce by half and thicken. Remove from the heat and set aside.

Peel the potatoes and cut into very fine even-sized dice – as small as you can. Place the diced potatoes into a pan of cold salted water, and over a medium heat bring to the boil and simmer until tender. Remove from the heat and drain thoroughly.

Bring a pan of unsalted water to the boil, drop in the samphire and blanch for 3 minutes. Refresh under cold running water, drain thoroughly and set aside.

Serves Four

275ml whipping cream
5 large Maris Piper potatoes
100g samphire, *carefully picked over,*
washed thoroughly
rapeseed oil
50g salted butter
2 shallots, *peeled, finely sliced*
1 garlic clove, *peeled, grated*
50g Parmesan, *freshly grated*
250g white crab meat
150ml chicken stock, *see page 236*
1 tbsp chopped parsley
1 tbsp snipped chives
1 tbsp chopped tarragon
sea salt & black pepper

Heat a large saucepan over a medium heat, add a splash of rapeseed oil and the butter with the shallots and garlic and cook until the shallots are softened but not coloured.

Add the potatoes to the shallots and garlic with the grated Parmesan, reduced whipping cream, and enough chicken stock until the sauce is thick enough to coat the back of a spoon – the sauce should cling to the spoon rather than run off. Carefully fold in the white crab meat so as not to break up the potato.

Just before serving fold in the chopped herbs and samphire and season with salt and freshly ground black pepper.

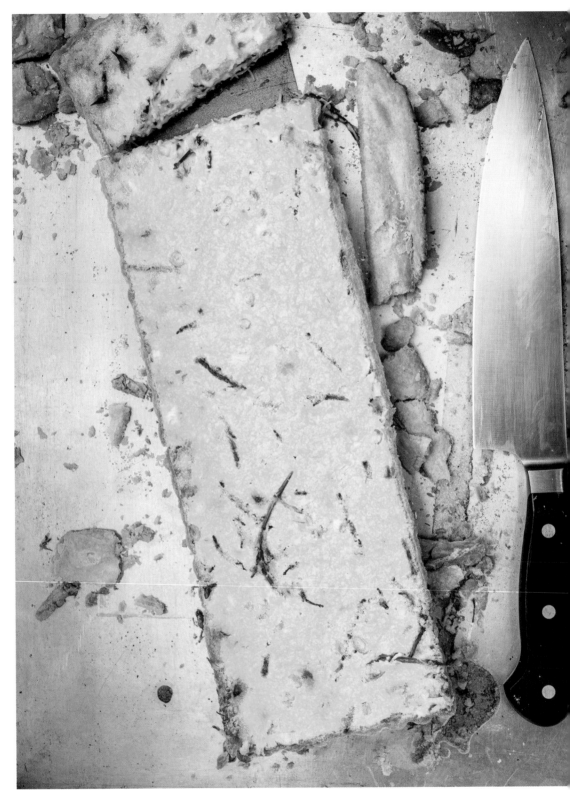

Stress-free

CRAB & BROWN SHRIMP TART

Serves Four

for the pastry:
250g plain flour
1 tsp salt
1 tsp sugar
150g salted butter, *softened*
1 egg, *beaten*

for the tart:
150g samphire,
carefully picked over, washed
5 eggs, *3 whole eggs, plus 2 egg yolks*
425ml whipping cream
1 pinch of freshly grated nutmeg
sea salt & black pepper
250g white crab meat
250g brown shrimps
40g Parmesan, *freshly grated*

For this recipe you'll need a fluted rectangular loose-based tart tin, roughly 36 x 12 x 3cm, and some baking beans.

To make the pastry, sift the flour onto a clean work surface and sprinkle over the salt and sugar. Make a well in the centre and add the softened butter with the beaten egg. Using your fingertips amalgamate the butter and egg until you achieve a scrambled egg consistency, then add a good splash of water and mix in. Draw in the flour, and again using your fingertips bring the pastry together. Wrap in cling film and refrigerate to rest.

When ready to use, remove the pastry from the fridge, roll out, and line the tart tin. Place on a baking tray and return to the fridge to rest for at least 1 hour.

To make the tart, preheat the oven to 180°C/350°F/gas mark 4. Cover the pastry-lined tart tin with baking parchment, fill with baking beans and place in the centre of the oven. Bake 'blind' for about 30 minutes, or until the pastry just starts to colour. Remove the baking beans and parchment: if there are any cracks in the pastry, use leftover pieces of pastry or beaten egg yolk to repair it. Return the pastry case to the oven for about 5 minutes, remove from the oven and leave to cool.

Bring a pan of unsalted water to the boil, drop in the samphire and blanch for 3 minutes. Refresh under cold running water and drain thoroughly. Pat dry on kitchen paper and set aside.

Place 3 eggs plus the 2 egg yolks and the whipping cream into a bowl and beat gently. Pass through a sieve into a pouring jug, season with nutmeg, salt and freshly ground black pepper and set aside.

When ready to cook the tart, heat the oven to 140°C/275°F/gas mark 1. Spread the samphire over the base of the cooked pastry case. Stir the white crab meat, brown shrimps and Parmesan into the egg mixture and carefully pour over the samphire. Place the tart on a baking tray in the centre of the preheated oven. Cook for about 50 minutes or until the filling is just set. Leave to cool for a few minutes before serving.

Serve slices of the tart with dressed salad leaves and some buttery new potatoes.

BARBECUED HAKE STEAKS/ NEW POTATOES

Scrape the potatoes, rinse and pat dry on kitchen paper. Place into a bowl with the garlic, olive oil, and season with salt and freshly ground pepper, mix thoroughly. Lay out 2 layers of foil paper on top of each other. Place the potatoes and garlic into the centre of the foil (pour over any olive oil from the bottom of the bowl), season, and scatter over the lavender stems. Gather up the foil to make a loose parcel and crimp the edges tightly together. Roast on the barbecue for about 40 minutes, until the potatoes are tender, watching carefully: you may need to shake them a little to get them evenly coloured.

Serves Four

900g new potatoes
8 garlic cloves
120ml olive oil
sea salt & black pepper
4 stems of lavender, *including leaves*
4 hake steaks, *brushed with olive oil*

About 10 minutes before the potatoes are ready carefully open the foil parcel, season the hake steaks and place on top of the potatoes. Gather up the foil and place back on the barbecue. After a few minutes open up the foil to allow the barbecue flavour to permeate through the steaks. The hake will be ready when the flesh starts to pull away easily.

LEMON SOLE WITH PARMESAN CRUST/ ASPARAGUS

Serves Four

for the Parmesan crust:
4 slices white bread,
semi-stale with crusts removed
150g Parmesan, *grated*
1 bunch of fresh parsley, *chopped*
4 tbsp melted butter
sea salt & black pepper

for the lemon sole:
2 lemon sole,
filleted to give 8 fillets
1 tbsp meat glue, *premium
quality transglutaminase*
100g melted butter, *for the fish
and for finishing the asparagus*
16 stalks of asparagus, *trimmed*

To make the Parmesan crust, place the stale bread, Parmesan, parsley, the 4 tablespoons of melted butter together with a good seasoning of salt and freshly ground black pepper into the bowl of a food processor. Blitz really well to form a cheesy crumb, and set aside.

To grill the lemon sole, lay 1 fillet out on your work surface, sprinkle a little meat glue over and place a matching fillet on top to form a thick fillet. Wrap firmly with cling film. Repeat to create 4 thick fillets, and refrigerate for at least 1 hour.

Preheat the oven to 180°C/350°F/gas mark 4. Remove the cling film from the fillets, dip each one into the melted butter and lay onto a greaseproof-covered baking tray. Liberally coat the top of each fillet with the cheesy crumb, place into the oven and bake for 6 minutes: the crust should be lightly coloured and bubbling.

At the same time bring a saucepan of salted water to the boil. Drop the asparagus into the boiling water and cook until just tender, but still retaining some bite. Drain the asparagus and toss in a little melted butter.

Serve the Parmesan-crusted fillet with a handful of asparagus sprinkled in sea salt.

LOBSTER/ BAKED PURPLE POTATOES & PARMESAN SAUCE

Serves Four

for the potatoes:

6 medium-sized purple potatoes,
such as Prairie Blush or Purple Majesty
olive oil
sea salt
100g salted butter
2 x 500g cooked lobsters,
meat removed, roughly diced

for the sauce:

250ml whipping cream
1 heaped tsp Dijon mustard
zest and juice of half a lemon
2 egg yolks
60g Parmesan, *grated*
2 tbsp chopped basil
1 pinch caster sugar
sea salt & black pepper

To bake the potatoes, preheat the oven to 200°C/400°F/gas mark 6. Wash the potatoes in cold water and then brush with a little oil and dust with sea salt to draw the moisture out of the skin. Bake the potatoes for 1-1¼ hours or until tender. Remove from the oven and set aside to cool slightly; when cool enough to handle, cut in half, scoop out the flesh, retaining the skin, and pass the flesh through a fine sieve into a saucepan, add the butter and mix through to incorporate thoroughly. Set aside and keep them warm.

To make the sauce, heat the cream, mustard, lemon zest and juice together in a pan until it comes to the boil. Take it off the heat, whisk in the egg yolks until combined, then stir in the Parmesan and add the basil. Season to taste with sugar, salt and freshly ground black pepper and continue to cook until the sauce thickens. Serve the sauce warm when needed.

To serve, increase the oven to 220°C/425°F/ gas mark 7. Divide the buttery potato mixture back into the potato skins and add the lobster and a spoonful of Parmesan sauce over the top. Bake in the oven for 3 to 4 minutes and serve immediately.

MUSSELS/
LOVAGE OIL
& PERRY

To make the lovage oil, bring a pan of water to the boil, drop in the 100g lovage and blanch for a couple of minutes. Immediately refresh in iced water, drain thoroughly and then squeeze dry in a clean tea towel until completely dry. Place in a blender with the grapeseed oil. Blend for 10 minutes and then pass through a muslin cloth, and set aside.

To cook the mussels, clean and scrub the mussels under cold running water, making sure all the beards are removed, and set aside.

Finely dice the vegetables and garlic, heat a pan over a moderate heat, add the butter and the diced vegetables and sweat until soft. Turn up the heat and throw in the mussels, add the perry, place a lid on the pan and cook the mussels for 2 minutes. Drain in a colander, retaining the cooking liquor and discarding any mussels which have not opened.

Pass the cooking liquor through a very fine sieve back into the pan and over a high heat boil to reduce by half. Add the cream, season with salt and freshly ground pepper, turn the heat down a little and reduce by a third. Add the mussels to the reduced sauce to heat right through.

Serve the mussels in the sauce garnished with remaining fresh lovage and the lovage oil.

Serves Four

for the lovage oil:
150g fresh lovage
200ml grapeseed oil

for the mussels:
2kg mussels
3 sticks celery
2 carrots, *peeled*
3 banana shallots, *peeled*
1 garlic clove, *peeled*
50g unsalted butter
300ml perry *(pear)* cider
100ml double cream
sea salt & black pepper

SALMON CEVICHE/ LIME MAYONNAISE

To marinate the salmon, lay a double layer of cling film on a tray allowing enough to wrap the salmon, and place the salmon in the middle. In a bowl, mix together the salt, 1 shallot, caster sugar, lemon zest and dill and rub into the salmon on both sides. Wrap the salmon in the cling film and refrigerate overnight.

An hour before serving unwrap the salmon and wash off the marinade under cold running water, then pat dry. Slice the salmon into 3cm wide strips, about 1cm thick, and lay them on a tray (chop the leftover salmon into chunks), sprinkle over the lemon juice, olive oil and freshly ground black pepper. Leave for half an hour before serving.

To make the mayonnaise, place 2 tablespoons of the lime juice into the bowl of a food processor with the white wine vinegar, egg and mustard powder. Season well with salt and freshly ground pepper, then whizz on a high speed until all the ingredients are combined. Slowly drizzle in the sunflower oil with the processor still running; the mixture will emulsify and gradually thicken. Add the lime zest and more lime juice if necessary. Check the seasoning and refrigerate until ready to use.

To serve, place a strip of salmon onto a plate, spoon over some pink grapefruit, chopped shallot, chopped salmon, coriander leaves and finish with lime mayonnaise.

Serves Four

for the salmon:
250g fillet of salmon, *skinned, pin-boned*
1 tbsp sea salt
2 shallots, *peeled, finely sliced*
1 tsp caster sugar
1 lemon, *grated zest of ½ lemon, juice of the whole lemon*
1 tbsp fresh chopped dill
2 tbsp olive oil
ground black pepper
1 pink grapefruit, *peeled, segmented*
1 handful of micro coriander

for the mayonnaise:
juice of 2 limes, *plus zest of 1 lime*
1 tbsp white wine vinegar
1 egg
1 tsp English mustard powder
275ml sunflower oil
sea salt & black pepper

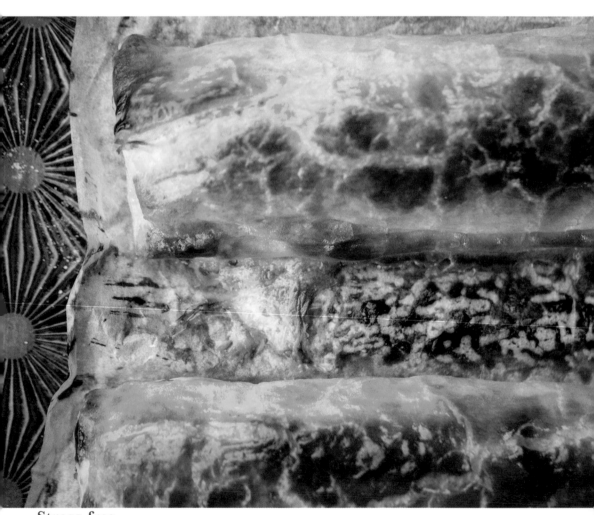

Stress-free

SALMON & GOATS' CHEESE ROLLS

To make the filling, mix the smoked salmon, goats' cheese, cream, lime juice and chives together in a bowl. Season with salt and freshly ground black pepper. Spoon the mixture into a piping bag and set aside.

Lay out a large piece of cling film on your work surface, pipe the smoked salmon mixture along the centre and roll up to form a long tight sausage shape. Chill in the fridge for at least 1 hour, until ready to use.

To make the rolls, preheat the oven to 200°C/400°F/gas mark 6. Bearing in mind the size of the salmon roll, roll out some pastry on a lightly floured surface to a thickness of about 5mm. Trim to create a straight edge. Unwrap the roll of salmon and place on the pastry along the straight edge. Brush the edges of the pastry with egg wash and roll the salmon up in the pastry to form a salmon roll, overlap the pastry and seal – it should look like a sausage roll.

Place on a baking tray lined with baking parchment and brush with egg wash. Bake in the preheated oven for 10 minutes.

Remove from the oven and allow to rest for a few minutes before slicing with a serrated knife and serving with a light fresh tomato salad.

Serves Four

for the filling:
275g smoked salmon, *very finely chopped*
150g goats' cheese, *cut into small dice*
6 tbsp double cream
juice of 1 lime
3 tbsp chopped chives
sea salt & black pepper

for the rolls:
350g all-butter puff pastry
2 egg yolks, *beaten*

CURED BLACKENED SALMON/ PICKLED CUCUMBER

To cure the salmon, combine the salt, sugar, coriander seeds, peppercorns, dill, orange juice and rind together in a bowl and then spread half of this mixture on a baking tray. Place the salmon on top, skin side down, cover with the remaining mixture, pour over the treacle and add the star anise. Cover with cling film and refrigerate for 24 hours. Remove from the fridge, turn the fish over, and spoon over the liquid which will be in the baking tray. Cover and return to the fridge to marinate for a further 24 hours.

After 48 hours the fish will be cured and should be carefully washed and patted dry. Once cured the salmon will keep for up to 1 week in the fridge wrapped tightly in cling film.

To make the pickled cucumber, place the vinegar and sugar into a saucepan and over a low heat allow the sugar to dissolve. Turn up the heat and bring to the boil, add the chilli, herbs, coriander seeds and white peppercorns, remove from the heat and leave to cool and infuse.

Peel the cucumber into thin strips and place into the cooled pickling liquor for at least 1 hour. When ready to serve, lift the cucumber out of the pickling liquor with a slotted spoon.

Serve wafer thin slices of salmon with the pickled cucumber and thinly sliced buttered brown bread.

Serves Four

for the salmon:
120g sea salt
90g soft dark brown sugar
1 tbsp coriander seeds, *crushed*
1 tbsp white peppercorns, *crushed*
6 tbsp chopped fresh dill
juice and rind of 1 orange
900g side of fresh salmon, *pin bones removed, skin descaled and left on*
60g black treacle
4 star anise

for the pickled cucumber:
250g cider vinegar
250g caster sugar
1 large red chilli, *finely sliced*
2 bay leaves
1 sprig tarragon
1 sprig thyme
1 tsp coriander seeds
½ tsp white peppercorns
2 cucumbers

"ONE OF MY SIMPLE PL
IS COOKING SEAFOOD
IF YOU COOK SCALLOPS
THE FIRE AND WAIT FO
OPEN IT IS ABSOLUTELY
IT'S A GREAT WAY TO
FIRST TIME"

EASURES AT HOME
ON A BARBECUE.
ON THE GRILL OVER
R THEIR SHELLS TO
INCREDIBLE.
TRY THEM FOR THE

Stress-free

BARBECUED SCALLOPS/ CHILLI DRESSING

Serves Four

for the dressing:
1 tbsp fresh ginger, *grated*
2 tbsp light soy sauce
2 tbsp sesame oil
2 tbsp rice wine vinegar
1 large red chilli, *finely sliced*
1 tsp honey
4 tbsp chopped coriander
1 tbsp garlic oil
juice of 1 lime
1 tbsp nam pla fish sauce
sea salt & black pepper

for the scallops:
12 king scallops, *3 per serving,
preferably in the shell; if not,
good clean scallops*
olive oil

To make the dressing, place all the ingredients into a large bowl and whisk well. Season with salt and freshly ground pepper, and set aside.

To cook the scallops, if using scallops out of their shell, make sure they are clean, dry and smeared with a little olive oil. Place the scallops onto the prepared barbecue and cook for about 2 minutes on each side. If you place the scallops onto the barbecue in their shells (they won't need smearing with olive oil) they will open in the most spectacular fashion: once opened leave them for another 2 minutes then take off the barbecue and remove the skirts (the frilly bit surrounding the scallop).

Serve whilst hot drizzled with chilli dressing.

PAN-FRIED SCALLOPS/ ROASTED VEGETABLES & NANTUA SAUCE

Serves Four

for the sauce:
80g salted butter
60g shallots, *peeled, finely sliced*
60g button mushrooms,
very finely sliced
500g shellfish shells and heads,
such as prawns or lobster, raw or
cooked, roughly chopped
2 tbsp Cognac
150ml dry white wine
300ml white fish stock,
see page 238
1 small bouquet garni,
half to be tarragon sprigs
80g ripe tomatoes, *peeled,*
cut and deseeded
1 pinch of cayenne pepper
sea salt & black pepper
300ml double cream
1 sprig tarragon, *finely snipped*

for the vegetables:
1 butternut squash
1 green courgette
1 yellow courgette
2 garlic cloves, *peeled, grated*
75ml olive oil
sea salt & black pepper

for the scallops:
12 king scallops, *3 per serving*
olive oil

To make the sauce, melt 40g of the butter in a large shallow saucepan over a low heat. Add the sliced shallots and mushrooms and sweat for 1 minute. Add the shellfish to the pan, increase the heat and fry briskly for 2 to 3 minutes, stirring continuously.

Pour in the Cognac and ignite with a match. Once the flames have died down, add the white wine and boil to reduce by half and then pour in the stock. Bring to the boil, and lower the heat so that the sauce bubbles gently. Add the bouquet garni, tomatoes, cayenne and a good pinch of salt and cook for 30 minutes.

Stir in the cream and let the sauce bubble for another 10 minutes. Pass through a fine sieve into another pan rubbing it through with the back of a ladle. Bring the sauce back to the boil, reduce if necessary and season with salt and freshly ground black pepper.

Remove from the heat and whisk in the rest of the butter a little at a time until the sauce is smooth and glossy, and set aside. When ready to serve, heat up and add the tarragon to enhance the flavour.

To roast the vegetables, preheat the oven to 200°C/400°F/gas mark 6. Peel and chop the butternut squash and courgettes chunkily. Place into a bowl with the grated garlic, olive oil and a good seasoning of salt and freshly ground black pepper. Mix thoroughly.

Lay a double layer of foil onto your work surface and place the vegetables in the centre. Draw up the sides of the foil to form a parcel and crimp the top. Place in the oven to roast. After 20 minutes have a look: the vegetables should be tender and brown around the edges. If they're not, give them a further 5 to 10 minutes. Remove from the oven and keep them warm

To fry the scallops, clean the scallops, remove the roes and membrane. Heat a frying pan until almost smoking hot, add a splash of olive oil and quickly fry the scallops for about 2 minutes on each side. The scallops should be no more than warm in the middle.

Serve the scallops on top of the vegetables and spoon over some warmed Nantua sauce.

Stress-free

CURRIED SCALLOPS/ TOMATO FONDUE, SAMPHIRE, PEACHES & CHILLI PAK CHOI

To cook the tomato fondue, sweat the shallot in olive oil in a pan until softened, add the garlic and tomatoes and stew down over a gentle heat. Season with salt and freshly ground pepper, and keep it warm.

To cook the samphire, bring a pan of unsalted water to the boil, drop in the samphire and blanch for 3 minutes. Refresh under cold running water, drain thoroughly and set aside.

To warm the peaches, when ready to serve; preheat the oven to 150°C/300°F/gas mark 2. Place the peaches onto a tray and into the oven to gently warm through for 8 minutes.

To cook the pak choi, when ready to serve, heat a frying pan over a high heat, add a good splash of groundnut oil and a splash of water, throw in the pak choi for 3 minutes, and when nearly cooked add the samphire and chillies to heat right through.

To cook the scallops, remove the roe and membrane from the scallops, wash carefully and pat dry. Smear a non-stick frying pan with olive oil and heat until hot. Roll the scallops in the curry powder to coat well, then place into the hot pan. Over a high heat sear the scallops for about 2 minutes on each side. The scallops will be warmed, but rare – if they're fresh this is the best way to eat them. If you prefer them cooked a little more, leave them in the pan for a little longer on each side.

To serve, place some samphire, peach slices, chilli and pak choi onto a plate, add a spoonful of the fondue and top with curried scallops.

Serves Four

for the tomato fondue:
1 shallot, *peeled, sliced*
2 tbsp olive oil
1 garlic clove, *peeled, finely sliced*
4 vine tomatoes,
peeled, deseeded, chopped
sea salt & black pepper

for the samphire, peaches and pak choi:
250g samphire,
carefully picked over, washed
3 ripe peaches,
stoned, skinned, sliced
groundnut oil
3 baby pak choi,
sliced in half lengthways
2 large red chillies,
sliced in half lengthways

for the scallops:
8 king scallops, *2 per serving*
olive oil
1 tbsp mild curry powder

TANDOORI SEA BASS/ RATATOUILLE

Serves Four

for the ratatouille:
2 red onions
1 large aubergine
2 yellow peppers
2 red peppers
2 courgettes
1 small fennel bulb
275 ml olive oil
1 garlic clove, *peeled, sliced*
sea salt & black pepper
250g baby vine tomatoes
25g basil, *roughly chopped*

for the marinade:
2 tbsp ginger and garlic paste,
4 garlic cloves, 1 small lobe of ginger,
peeled, grated, and 3 tbsp vegetable oil,
blended to a paste
1 tsp cracked black pepper
$\frac{1}{2}$ tsp garam masala powder
1 tbsp ground coriander
$\frac{1}{2}$ tsp cumin powder
$\frac{1}{2}$ tsp red chilli powder
2 tbsp rapeseed oil
1 tbsp lemon juice
8 tbsp plain yoghurt

for the sea bass:
4 fillets of wild sea bass, *descaled,*
skin left on, pin bones removed
sea salt & black pepper

To make the ratatouille, preheat the oven to 220°C/425°F/gas mark 7. Peel the onions, cut into quarters and then cut each quarter lengthways again. Roughly chop the remaining vegetables, and put into a large bowl with the onions. Pour over the olive oil, add the garlic, and mix thoroughly with your hands. Spread out the vegetables in a roasting tin and season with salt and freshly ground black pepper.

Place in the oven. Once the vegetables have started to colour add the tomatoes and basil. Mix well and cook for 20 minutes, until the vegetables are well coloured, but are still reasonably crunchy. Check the seasoning and serve either warmed through or cold.

To make the marinade, mix all the ingredients together in a bowl until combined. Place the fillets of sea bass into a dish, pour over the marinade and using your fingers rub it into the fish. Set aside to marinate for 30 minutes.

To barbecue the sea bass, lift the sea bass from the marinade and place skin side down onto the prepared barbecue. Season with salt and freshly ground black pepper and cook for about 5 minutes, remove carefully and serve immediately with the ratatouille.

Stress-free

SEA TROUT WRAP/
MUSTARD VINAIGRETTE

Serves Four

for the vinaigrette:
2 tbsp red wine vinegar
1 tsp Dijon mustard
1 tsp clear honey
1 garlic clove, *peeled, finely sliced*
175ml extra virgin olive oil
a squeeze of fresh lemon juice
1 small shallot, *peeled, finely sliced*
sea salt & black pepper

for the sea trout:
350g sea trout,
filleted. skinned, pin-boned
rapeseed oil
sea salt & black pepper
1 iceberg lettuce,
broken into cup-shaped leaves
2 Braeburn apples,
unpeeled, cut into batons
2 pink grapefruit, *peeled, segmented*

To make the vinaigrette, in a bowl whisk together the vinegar, Dijon mustard, honey and garlic. Slowly add the oil, whisking continuously, then stir in the lemon juice and shallot, season with salt and freshly ground black pepper and set aside.

To cook the sea trout, preheat the oven to 100°C/210°F/gas mark ¼. Place the sea trout onto a baking tray, drizzle over a little rapeseed oil and season with salt and a good grinding of black pepper. Place into the oven and cook for about 5 minutes, until the flesh is just starting to come away. Remove from the oven, set aside and allow to cool.

To serve, build a cup shape with lettuce leaves, add apple and segments of pink grapefruit, then flake some sea trout over the top and drizzle with vinaigrette. Simple, but so fresh and more-ish!

DUCK EGG WITH BROWN SHRIMPS & COCKLES/ SOURDOUGH TOAST

Preheat the oven to 180°C/350°F/gas mark 4. Gently heat 4 small ovenproof frying pans on the hob. Add a knob of butter to each, and when it starts to foam crack a duck egg into each pan. Fry until the egg whites start to set. Scatter over the shrimps and cockles and put the pans into the oven to carry on cooking the yolks: be careful not to overcook them – keep them nice and runny.

Remove the pans from the oven, sprinkle with chopped parsley and smoked paprika.

Serve with the toasted sourdough bread.

Serves Four

4 knobs of salted butter
4 free-range duck eggs
100g brown shrimps, *cooked, peeled*
100g cockles, *cooked*
2 tbsp chopped parsley
2 tbsp smoked paprika
4 slices of chunky sourdough,
toasted to serve

Stress-free

BROWN SHRIMP RISOTTO

Heat the chicken stock in a pan over a low heat.

In a separate saucepan, melt the butter and gently sauté the shallots. Add the rice and, stirring continuously, cook for a few minutes. Add the white wine and cook until evaporated.

Start stirring in the hot stock, a ladleful at a time, adding the next ladleful only when most of the stock has been absorbed – don't try to rush as time is of the essence for a really successful risotto: it should take at least 20 minutes to absorb the stock. The risotto is ready when it is creamy in texture but not chalky, and the grains still retain a little 'bite'. You may not need all the stock, but it's better to have it ready just in case.

When the risotto is nearly ready, and the stock is absorbed, stir in the brown shrimps and white crab meat, making sure they are fully warmed through. Finally stir in the petis pois, Parmesan and mascarpone together with the chilli and coriander. Season well with salt and freshly ground black pepper and allow to stand for a couple of minutes. A really good risotto should fall into the shape of the bowl when served, and not just stay in a solid lump.

Serve with a crisp chilled glass of Sancerre and some crusty sourdough bread.

Serves Four

1.2 litres chicken stock, *see page 236*
50g salted butter
2 shallots, *peeled, finely sliced*
250g Arborio risotto rice
4 tbsp white wine
250g brown shrimps
125g white crab meat
75g petis pois
100g fresh Parmesan, *grated*
1 dollop of mascarpone cheese
2 tbsp mild red chilli, *finely sliced*
4 tbsp chopped fresh coriander
sea salt & black pepper

CREVETTE
JOHN DO
OYSTERS/T
RED SNAPP
SC

*With a little mild heat

SPICY SEAFOOD*

CREVETTES À LA PLANCHA

Mix the chopped parsley, chilli and garlic in a bowl and combine with enough olive oil to make a paste runny enough to coat the crevettes.

Serves Four

1 handful of chopped parsley
1 large mild red chilli,
deseeded, finely sliced
3 garlic cloves, *peeled, crushed*
olive oil
16 large fresh crevettes,
or shell-on prawns
2 lemons, *cut into wedges*

Marinate the crevettes in the paste for at least 1 hour before serving.

Heat a plancha or griddle pan until hot.

Remove the crevettes from the marinade, place on the hot plancha and cook for about 2 minutes on each side, depending on how big they are, until they turn pink and are cooked right through.

Serve immediately with freshly squeezed lemon.

Spicy seafood

Spicy seafood

154 — 155

SPICY FISH SOUP/ GRILLED RED MULLET & ROUILLE

Serves Four

for the fish soup:
1kg Mediterranean fish,
such as red mullet or gurnard, filleted
1 pinch of saffron
1 pinch of cayenne
rapeseed oil
90g carrot, *peeled, finely chopped*
20g celery, *finely chopped*
80g onion, *peeled, finely chopped*
20g fennel, *finely chopped*
1 red chilli, *finely chopped*
80g red pepper, *finely chopped*
25g leek, *finely sliced*
1/2 garlic clove, *peeled, grated*
1 bay leaf
1 sprig of thyme
40ml Pernod
20ml Armagnac
100g plum tomatoes, *deseeded*
60g tomato purée
1 litre brown fish stock and
1 litre white fish stock,
see page 238
sea salt & black pepper
roasted tomatoes, *see page 32*
basil oil, *see page 236*
1 handful of micro parsley leaves

for the rouille:
1 egg yolk
1 garlic clove, *peeled, finely sliced*
1/2 tsp harissa paste
1 pinch of saffron
85g olive oil
85g vegetable oil
50g dry mashed potato

for the red mullet:
4 fillets of red mullet,
pin-boned, descaled
olive oil
sea salt & black pepper

To make the fish soup, skin and fillet the fish. Cut into decent-sized chunks and then rub the fish with the saffron and cayenne. Cover and refrigerate for 12 hours to marinate.

Preheat the oven to 180°C/350°F/gas mark 4. Remove the fish from the marinade and place it onto a baking tray in the oven to roast for 1 hour.

Heat a large saucepan, add a splash of rapeseed oil and all the vegetables, garlic, bay leaf and thyme. Sweat off the vegetables until lightly caramelised. Add the Pernod and Armagnac and scrape the pan to deglaze. Add the baked fish, tomatoes, tomato purée and fish stocks, and simmer for 30 minutes. Liquidise and pass through a fine sieve. Check the consistency, reduce a little if you like it thicker, and set aside.

To make the rouille, whisk the egg yolk, garlic, harissa and saffron together in a bowl. Combine the 2 oils and then while vigorously whisking the egg yolk mixture, very slowly drip in the oils to form a mayonnaise. Finally whisk in the potato and then pass through a sieve, and set aside.

To grill the red mullet, heat the grill to high. Place the 4 red mullet fillets skin side up on a baking tray which has been brushed with olive oil, season the flesh side with salt and freshly ground black pepper then grill the mullet for 2 to 3 minutes until the flesh is just cooked and the skin has a good crispness.

To serve, heat the soup so that it is piping hot, season with salt and freshly ground pepper, and ladle into bowls. Add the grilled red mullet, roasted tomatoes and a couple of drops of rouille and basil oil. Garnish with micro parsley and serve with some crusty sourdough bread.

JOHN DORY/
LEMONGRASS, GINGER & CHILLI

Serves Four

1 whole John Dory,
roughly 1.5kg, head removed
4 sticks lemongrass
50g fresh ginger, *peeled*
1 large mild red chilli
2 shallots, *peeled*
2 heads fennel
1 stick celery
1 handful coriander stalks
300ml rice wine vinegar
300ml sake
150ml mirin
150ml double cream
100g salted butter
sea salt & black pepper
1 red chilli, *finely sliced for garnish*
1 small bunch of coriander,
roughly chopped for garnish

Preheat the oven to 160°C/325°F/gas mark 3.
Clean and wipe the John Dory and set aside.

Finely slice the lemongrass, ginger, chilli, shallots,
fennel and celery and spread on a baking tray;
scatter the coriander stalks over the vegetables.

Place the fish on top of the vegetables and pour
over the rice wine vinegar, sake and mirin.
Place into the preheated oven to bake for 15
minutes. Insert a toothpick into the thickest part
of the fish – if cooked, it should slip in easily;
if not return the fish to the oven for a further
5 minutes. Set the fish aside and keep it warm.

While the fish is resting strain the cooking liquor
into a saucepan and over a high heat bring to
the boil and reduce by half. Add the cream and
continue to reduce. Finally whisk in the butter and
season with salt and freshly ground black pepper.

Remove the fillets from the fish and serve with
the sauce. Garnish with chilli and coriander.

Spicy seafood

SPICED MONKFISH/ SAFFRON RICE

To make the rice, preheat the oven to 180°C/350°F/gas mark 4. Melt the butter in a heavy-based saucepan. Add the shallots and garlic and fry gently until soft and translucent. Stir in the rice and saffron and continue to gently cook for a further few minutes. Next, pour in 600ml of the stock and add the thyme. Bring to simmering point, cover the pan with greaseproof paper and place in the preheated oven for 40 minutes. After 20 minutes check the texture of the rice: if it looks as if it might become a little dry, add some more of the stock.

After 40 minutes the rice should be cooked and will have absorbed most of the liquid. Season with salt and freshly ground black pepper and the rice is ready to serve. It can be warmed through when needed.

To cook the monkfish, preheat the oven to 180°C/350°F/gas mark 4. Coat the monkfish with the ras el hanout powder. Heat an ovenproof dish large enough to take the monkfish tail on a medium heat and add a good splash of rapeseed oil. Place the fish in the pan to seal and colour, turning and seasoning with salt and freshly ground black pepper as you do so. Transfer to the oven and roast for about 20 minutes. Remove from the oven and set aside somewhere warm to rest for about 5 minutes.

Carve the meat off the bone, and serve with the saffron rice and the curry sauce.

Serves Four

for the rice:
75g salted butter
2 large shallots, *peeled, finely sliced*
1 garlic clove, *peeled, finely sliced*
250g long grain rice
1 pinch of saffron,
infused in 2 tbsp boiling water
850ml chicken stock, *see page 236*
1 sprig of fresh thyme
4 tbsp chopped chives
sea salt & black pepper

for the monkfish:
1 large whole monkfish tail,
*roughly 1kg, trimmed, all
membrane removed*
1 tbsp ras el hanout powder
rapeseed oil
sea salt & black pepper
Sauternes and curry sauce,
see page 180

"SEAFOOD IS PARTICU[LARLY]
ON OTHER FLAVOURS —
AND SPICE HAVE AN E[X]
YOU SEE THIS AT ITS B[EST]
PART OF THE REASON
TO HELP KEEP FOOD T[ASTING]
CLIMATES — BUT MA[YBE]
TASTE SO GOOD TOGET[HER]

ARLY GOOD AT TAKING
OR ME SEAFOOD
TRA SPECIAL AFFINITY.
ST IN THE FAR EAST.
FOR THE PAIRING IS
STING FRESH IN HOT
NLY BECAUSE THEY
HER"

BARBECUE OYSTERS/ CHILLI DRESSING

Serves Four

12 oysters, *3 per serving*

for the dressing:
2 tbsp Chardonnay wine vinegar
2 tbsp rice wine
juice of half a lemon
1 shallot, *peeled, very finely diced*
1 tsp green chilli, *finely sliced*
1 tsp red chilli, *finely sliced*
sea salt & black pepper
150ml olive oil
1 tsp snipped chives

To make the dressing, in a bowl whisk together the Chardonnay vinegar, rice wine, lemon juice, shallot and chillies with a good seasoning of salt and freshly ground black pepper. While continuing to whisk, slowly add the olive oil. Just before serving, stir in the snipped chives and check the seasoning.

To serve, place the oysters in their shells onto the prepared barbecue and cook for about 1 minute until they open – when they do (discard any that don't), remove from the barbecue, pour in a teaspoon of the dressing and serve immediately.

Spicy seafood

SOUTHERN-FRIED OYSTERS/
PICKLED CUCUMBER & DILL EMULSION

Serves Four

for the pickled cucumber:
½ cucumber
½ large red chilli
100ml white wine vinegar
100g caster sugar
1 tbsp chopped dill
sea salt & black pepper

for the emulsion:
1 bunch fresh dill,
plus extra for garnishing
100ml grapeseed oil
2 tsp of Dijon mustard
2 egg yolks
sea salt & black pepper

for the oysters:
8 oysters, *2 per serving*
150g plain flour
2 tsp garlic powder
3 tsp smoked paprika
3 tsp celery salt
1 tsp turmeric
1 litre vegetable oil, *for frying*

To make the pickled cucumber, peel the cucumber, cut in half lengthways, remove the seeds and cut into fine dice. Cut the chilli in half, remove the seeds and cut into fine dice. Mix the vinegar, sugar and chopped dill in a bowl and add the cucumber and chilli. Season with salt and freshly ground black pepper and set aside.

To make the emulsion, place the dill and grapeseed oil into a blender, blitz really well and pass through a fine sieve into a jug. Whisk the mustard and egg yolks together in a bowl and while continuing to vigorously whisk, very slowly drip in the dill oil to emulsify into a mayonnaise consistency. Season with salt and freshly ground pepper, cover and set aside.

To fry the oysters, heat the oil in a deep fat fryer to 180°C/350°F/gas mark 4. Shuck the oysters and make sure all the shell has been removed along with any excess oyster juice. Clean the shells thoroughly and set aside. Mix the flour, garlic powder, paprika, salt and turmeric together, and roll the oysters in the mix making sure they are completely covered. Deep fry for 3 to 4 minutes until golden and crispy, remove and drain on kitchen paper.

Serve the oysters in the cleaned shells with some drained pickled cucumber and dill emulsion. Garnish with fresh sprigs of dill.

TIGER PRAWN & POTATO CURRY/ SAMPHIRE & BROAD BEANS

Serves Four

55g salted butter
2 large shallots, *peeled, finely sliced*
150g button mushrooms,
finely sliced
35g plain flour
2 tbsp mild curry powder
300ml Sauternes white wine
600ml white fish stock,
see page 238
150ml double cream
sea salt & black pepper
225g samphire,
carefully picked over, washed
500g medium-sized new potatoes,
scraped, quartered
175g smoked streaky bacon,
chopped into lardons
olive oil
125g broad beans, *skins removed*
12 large tiger prawns,
3 per serving, peeled
2 lemons, *cut into wedges*

Melt the butter in a heavy-based saucepan, add the shallots and mushrooms, sauté until softened but not coloured. Add the flour and curry powder and continue to cook for a further 4 to 5 minutes, stirring continuously.

Pour in the Sauternes, scrape the pan well, turn up the heat a little and bubble to reduce by a third. Add the fish stock, bring to a gentle simmer and cook for roughly 30 minutes, whisking occasionally, until the sauce is thick enough to coat the back of a spoon – the sauce should cling to the spoon rather than run off. Add the cream, check the consistency again, season with salt and freshly ground pepper, and then pass through a sieve and set aside.

Bring a pan of unsalted water to the boil, drop in the samphire and blanch for 30 seconds. Refresh under cold running water, drain thoroughly and set aside.

Place the new potatoes in a large saucepan of cold salted water, bring to the boil and cook for 25 minutes until just tender.

While the potatoes are boiling, heat a large frying pan and fry the chopped bacon in a little olive oil. Drain and slice the new potatoes and add them to the bacon, turn to colour all over, then add the curry sauce, samphire and broad beans.

To serve, throw in the prawns, cook for about 5 minutes until just cooked through, season with salt and freshly ground black pepper and serve immediately with the lemon wedges.

Spicy seafood

Spicy seafood

TIGER PRAWN & NOODLE BROTH

Serves Four

12 shell-on raw king prawns
rapeseed oil
3 garlic cloves, *peeled, grated*
1 carrot, *peeled, finely sliced*
1 large lobe of ginger, *peeled, grated*
2 sticks of lemongrass, *chopped*
2 bird's-eye chillies, *deseeded,*
1 finely chopped, the other
sliced into fine rings
3 lime leaves
1 tbsp palm sugar
1 star anise
1 tbsp tomato paste
800ml chicken stock,
see page 236
nam pla fish sauce, *to taste*
juice of 1 lime
sea salt & black pepper
300g rice noodles
12 tbsp vegetable oil
100g mange tout, *sliced*
100g beansprouts
4 spring onions, *finely sliced*
1 handful of coriander and
mint leaves, *roughly chopped*
2 limes, *cut into wedges*

Peel the prawns, remove and reserve the heads and shells and set aside.

Heat a medium-sized pan over a moderate heat, add a splash of rapeseed oil and throw in the prawn shells and heads, sauté for a couple of minutes until they turn pink. Add the garlic, carrot, ginger, lemon grass and the finely chopped chilli, together with the lime leaves, palm sugar, star anise and tomato paste. Continue to sauté until golden brown in colour. Add the fish or chicken stock, bring to the boil, turn down the heat and simmer for 20 minutes.

Strain the contents of the pan through a fine sieve lined with muslin into another pan.

Place the pan on the heat, bring to a boil and simmer to reduce by about half to intensify the flavour. Season with the fish sauce, lime juice, salt and freshly ground black pepper. Add 200g rice noodles and the prawns and continue to simmer until the noodles are cooked and the prawns are pink and tender.

In a large saucepan heat the vegetable oil over high heat, carefully drop the remaining rice noodles into the hot oil and cook for 1 minute. Remove the noodles and drain on kitchen paper.

Serve the broth in bowls, garnished with mange tout, beansprouts, fried rice noodles, spring onions, the sliced chilli, coriander, mint and freshly squeezed lime juice.

TIGER PRAWN & POTATO FRITTERS/
VIETNAMESE DIPPING SAUCE

Serves Four

for the dipping sauce:
250ml water
2 tbsp white wine vinegar
4 tbsp lime juice
1 chilli, *deseeded, finely sliced*
3 garlic cloves, *peeled, grated*
1 small lobe of ginger,
peeled, grated
8 tbsp nam pla fish sauce
4 tbsp caster sugar

for the fritters:
750g self-raising flour
750ml sparkling water
½ tsp salt
½ tsp caster sugar
½ tsp turmeric
3 large Maris Piper potatoes
12 raw tiger prawns, *3 per serving*
1 litre vegetable oil, *for frying*
8 spring onions, *chopped*
1 handful of coriander, *chopped*

To make the dipping sauce, whisk all the ingredients together in a bow. Set aside until needed.

To make the fritters, in a bowl mix together the flour, sparkling water, salt, sugar and turmeric and set aside to rest for 10 minutes.

Peel the potatoes and cut into julienne strips. Peel and devein the tiger prawns and cut in half lengthways. Set aside.

Heat the oil in a deep fat fryer to 180°C. Fold the potatoes, prawns, spring onions and coriander through the batter mix. Using your hands, shape them into fritters, making sure you have an even distribution of prawns in each fritter. Lower them into the hot oil and fry until crisp and golden brown. Remove from the fryer and drain well on kitchen paper.

Serve immediately with the dipping sauce.

Spicy seafood

Spicy seafood

BAKED WHOLE RED SNAPPER/ MANGO & AVOCADO SALSA

Serves Four

for the salsa:
2 red peppers
2 avocados, *peeled, sliced*
6 tbsp olive oil
juice of 2 limes
1 large red chilli, *finely sliced*
sea salt & black pepper
1 ripe mango, *peeled,*
cut into small dice
1 medium red onion,
peeled, finely sliced
3 vine tomatoes, *peeled,*
deseeded, finely sliced
1/2 cucumber, *peeled,*
deseeded, finely sliced
3 tbsp finely chopped coriander
2 tbsp finely chopped mint
nam pla fish sauce, *optional*

for the red snapper:
1 whole red snapper, *roughly 2kg,*
descaled, gutted, head left on
10 tbsp mayonnaise
2 small fiery red chillies,
finely sliced
1 garlic clove, *peeled, grated*
1 tsp ground cumin
4 tbsp olive oil
4 tbsp lime juice
1 tbsp sea salt

To make the salsa, roast the peppers whole, remove the skins and discard. Slice the peppers into strips and place into a large bowl with the avocados, olive oil, lime juice and chilli. Season with salt and freshly ground pepper, mix well, then add all the other ingredients. Check the seasoning, adding a little more lime juice if needed, and set aside. If you're not using the salsa straight away, cover the surface with cling film, then cover the top of the bowl again tightly to keep the air out and prevent any discolouring.

To bake the red snapper, lay the whole fish onto a baking tray. Mix the mayonnaise, chillies, garlic, cumin, olive oil, lime juice and sea salt in a bowl, smear over the fish and leave to marinate for 1 hour.

Preheat the oven to 180°C/350°F/gas mark 4. Bake the fish in the preheated oven for 25 to 30 minutes, basting occasionally.

Remove the fish from the oven, fillet, and serve with the salsa and some buttery new potatoes.

FRUITY SEAFOOD CURRY

Serves Four

for the curry sauce:
40g salted butter
60g onions, *peeled, sliced*
300g pineapple,
skinned, cut into small pieces
1 banana, *peeled, cut into rounds*
1 Cox's dessert apple,
skin on, chopped
25g medium curry powder
2 tbsp desiccated coconut
300ml chicken stock, *see page 236*
200ml coconut milk
sea salt & black pepper
2 tbsp mild curry powder,
275g monkfish tail, *membrane
removed, cut into 2.5cm cubes*
275g salmon fillet, *skin removed,
cut into 2.5cm cubes*
6 king scallops, *sliced
in half horizontally*
garlic oil
450g shell-on cooked prawns,
remove the shells yourself
4 tbps chopped coriander
rapeseed oil
1 bunch of spring onions,
trimmed, finely sliced
250g of baby leaf spinach
saffron rice, *see page 159*
1 handful of micro coriander

Melt the butter in a saucepan, add the onions and sweat over a low heat to soften. Add the pineapple, banana and apple and cook gently for 5 minutes. Stir in the curry powder and coconut, and pour in the chicken stock and coconut milk. Bring to the boil and simmer for 20 minutes.

Pass the curry sauce through a fine sieve, season with salt and freshly ground pepper, and set aside covered with cling film (pressed down to prevent a skin forming).

Place the mild curry powder onto a plate and lightly dust the monkfish, salmon and scallops and set aside.

Heat a frying pan on a medium heat, add a good splash of garlic oil followed by the pieces of monkfish, turning as you do so to colour lightly. Remove from the pan and place in another large saucepan. Repeat with the salmon and scallops and add to the monkfish together with the peeled prawns.

Pour the curry sauce over the seafood and bring to a simmer over a medium heat. Cook for about 5 minutes until the seafood is just cooked through, then add the coriander.

While the seafood is cooking, heat a large frying pan until hot, add a good splash of rapeseed oil and the spring onions and fry for 1 minute before adding the spinach: cook long enough to just wilt the spinach.

Add the spinach and spring onions to the curry and serve with saffron rice, garnish with micro coriander leaves.

Spicy seafood

Spicy seafood

SEA TROUT & CHILLI DUMPLINGS/ JAPANESE DIPPING SAUCE

Serves Four

for the dumplings:
300g sea trout fillet, *skinned, pin bones removed*
1 large red chilli, *deseeded, finely sliced*
6 spring onions, *sliced*
1 small lobe of ginger, *peeled, grated*
1 tbsp soy sauce
1 tsp sesame oil
2 tbsp chopped coriander
sea salt & black pepper
12 dumpling wrappers
1 large red chilli, *sliced for garnish*
4 spring onions, *sliced for garnish*
1 handful of micro coriander

for the dipping sauce:
2 tbsp olive oil
1 tbsp sesame oil
1 small onion, *peeled, finely sliced*
1 garlic clove, *crushed*
1 small lobe of ginger, *peeled, grated*
1 large red chilli, *deseeded, finely sliced*
50g soft dark brown sugar
150ml dark soy sauce
50ml sake
150ml mirin
sea salt & black pepper

To make the dipping sauce, heat the oils in a pan over a medium heat, add the onion, garlic and ginger, and sauté. Add the chilli and continue to sauté, then add the sugar, soy sauce, sake and the mirin. Bring to a simmer then lower the heat and allow the sauce to bubble and reduce to a fairly thick consistency. Strain the sauce and season with salt and freshly ground black pepper and set aside.

To make the dumplings, slice and then finely dice the sea trout and place into a bowl with the chilli, spring onions, ginger, soy sauce, sesame oil and chopped coriander. Season with salt and freshly ground black pepper and bind together.

Lay the dumpling wrappers out on your work surface and place a large teaspoon of the trout mixture in the centre. Dip your fingers into a little cold water and dampen round the edge of the dumpling wrapper. Fold the wrapper over and press to seal the damp edges together, then draw in each end and press to seal, making a small parcel. Steam the dumplings in a double boiler for 5 minutes.

Serve the dumplings with the dipping sauce, and a handful of sliced chilli, spring onion and micro coriander leaves scattered over the top.

ROASTED SCALLOPS/ SAUTERNES & CURRY SAUCE WITH CAULIFLOWER

Serves Four

for the cauliflower:
1 medium sized cauliflower
75g salted butter
150ml double cream
juice of 1 lemon
sea salt & black pepper
150g salted butter, *softened*

for the curry sauce:
55g salted butter
2 large shallots, *peeled, finely sliced*
35g plain flour
1 tbsp mild curry powder
150g button mushrooms,
finely sliced
100ml Sauternes white wine
300ml white fish stock,
see page 238
75ml double cream
sea salt & black pepper

for the scallops:
8 king scallops, *2 per serving,
cleaned, roe removed*
olive oil
sea salt & black pepper

To prepare the cauliflower, remove the outer green leaves and break the white florets into pieces, retaining 8 florets for frying. Melt 75g butter in a saucepan and add the broken florets, turn the heat down and place a lid on the pan, cook until the cauliflower is really tender. Take the lid off the pan, and over a moderate heat start to caramelise the cauliflower, once well browned all over add the cream and the lemon juice. Put the cauliflower and juice into a blender and blitz until you get a really light, smooth purée. Check the seasoning and transfer to a pan, keep warm until needed.

To make the curry sauce, melt the butter in a heavy-based saucepan, add the shallots and sauté until softened but not coloured. Add the flour and curry powder and continue to cook for a further 4 to 5 minutes, stirring continuously.

Add the mushrooms and cook for a couple of minutes before stirring in the white wine. Scrape the pan well, turn up the heat a little and bubble to reduce by a third. Add the fish stock, bring to a gentle simmer and cook for a further 30 minutes or so, whisking occasionally, until the sauce is thick enough to coat the back of a spoon – the sauce should cling to the spoon rather than run off. Add the cream, check the consistency again, season with salt and freshly ground pepper, and then pass through a sieve and set aside.

When ready to serve, place the 8 retained cauliflower florets and the softened butter into a frying pan, gently fry and caramelise the florets in the butter, turning occasionally until the cauliflower is cooked through. Lightly season with salt and freshly ground black pepper and keep warm.

To cook the scallops, heat a frying pan over a high heat, and add a splash of olive oil. Add the scallops, season well with salt and freshly ground black pepper and press down firmly. Fry for about 2 minutes on each side to achieve a deep roasted colour.

To serve, spread cauliflower purée onto a plate, add a couple of roasted scallops and cauliflower florets, and drizzle with the curry sauce.

Spicy seafood

Spicy seafood

PAN-FRIED SCALLOPS/ CHORIZO WITH SPINACH & QUAILS' EGGS

Heat a large frying pan and smear with a little rapeseed oil, then fry the chorizo, turning as you do so until coloured on both sides – the chorizo will release a lot of flavoured oil, which will add flavour to the spinach.

When the chorizo is nearly ready, throw in the spinach and continue to fry and wilt the spinach. Remove the chorizo and spinach from the pan and set aside.

Turn up the heat and add another splash of rapeseed oil to the same pan and fiercely fry the scallops: this will take about 1 minute.

Turn down the heat and add the chorizo and spinach back into the pan and break in the quails' eggs. Cook for a further minute or so, season with salt and freshly ground pepper and serve immediately.

Serves Four

rapeseed oil
2 small chorizo sausages, *sliced*
75g baby spinach, *washed*
24 queen scallops, *6 per serving*
8 quails' eggs, *2 per serving*
sea salt & black pepper

CURRIED SCALLOPS/ GUJARATI CARROT SALAD

Serves Four

for the salad:
2 medium carrots
4 limes, *juiced*
1 tsp sugar
1 tsp salt
3 tbsp vegetable oil
1 tsp black onion seeds
1 tsp yellow mustard seeds
1 handful of coriander cress

for the scallops:
8 king scallops, *2 per serving cleaned, roe removed*
1 tbsp mild curry powder
1 tsp caster sugar
1 tsp salt
olive oil

To make the salad, peel the carrots and slice thinly using a mandoline to about the width of matchsticks, place in a bowl with the lime juice, sugar and salt and mix thoroughly.

Heat the oil in a pan over a moderate heat, add the onion and mustard seeds and cook until the seeds start to sizzle, then pour over the carrots, mix well and set aside.

To cook the scallops, remove the membrane from the scallops, and clean thoroughly.

Combine the curry powder, sugar and salt in a bowl, and then roll the scallops in the mix and coat the scallops all over.

Heat a pan and add a splash of olive oil, place the scallops into the pan and sauté for about 2 minutes on each side until they are golden brown, firm to the touch, and cooked through.

To serve, mix some of the coriander cress through the salad, retaining some for garnish. Serve the salad with the scallops and garnish with the remaining coriander cress, and drizzle with any leftover dressing from the salad.

Spicy seafood

Spicy seafood

SQUID IN BLACK BEAN SAUCE/ DEEP-FRIED SHALLOTS

Serves Four

for the shallots:
75g seasoned plain flour
1 egg, *whisked with 4 tbsp milk*
150g Panko breadcrumbs
2 shallots, *peeled, sliced into rings*
1 litre vegetable oil, *for frying*

for the squid:
350g baby squid
1 tbsp cornflour
1 tbsp sesame oil
rapeseed oil
1 tbsp rice wine
1 tbsp soy sauce
2 shallots, *peeled, finely sliced*
2 garlic cloves, *peeled, grated*
6 tbsp cooked black beans, *rinsed*
1 lobe of ginger, *peeled, grated*
1 tbsp soy sauce
1 tbsp sesame oil
250ml chicken stock, *see page 236*
1 good pinch of sugar
sea salt & black pepper
1 tbsp chopped mint
2 tbsp chopped coriander
1 large red chilli, *sliced*
2 tbsp sliced spring onions
juice of 2 limes

To prepare the shallots, place the seasoned flour onto a plate, put the egg and milk into a shallow bowl and the Panko breadcrumbs onto another plate. Dust the shallot rings with the seasoned flour, dip into the beaten egg, shaking off any excess as you lift them out, and then coat with the Panko breadcrumbs. Set aside on kitchen paper.

To cook the squid, wash the squid, separating the tubes from the tentacles and set aside.

Mix the cornflour, sesame oil, 2 tablespoons of rapeseed oil, rice wine and soy sauce together in a bowl, add the squid and coat well. Cover and refrigerate for up to 3 hours.

Heat a frying pan or wok over a high heat and add a good splash of rapeseed oil. Remove the squid from the marinade and add to the pan and stir-fry for a couple of minutes. Using a slotted spoon remove the squid from the pan and set aside on kitchen paper.

Add another splash of rapeseed oil to the same pan, turn the heat down, add the shallots and garlic and sauté until softened but not coloured. Next add the black beans and ginger with the soy sauce, sesame oil, chicken stock and a good pinch of sugar. Turn up the heat a little and bring the mixture up to simmering point.

Return the squid to the pan and cook for a further 5 minutes or so, tasting and seasoning with salt and freshly ground black pepper as you do so.

To fry the shallots, as the squid is returned to the pan heat the oil in a deep fat fryer to 180°C. Carefully lower the shallots into the oil and fry until crisp and golden brown. Remove from the fryer and drain on kitchen paper.

Serve the squid in the black bean sauce topped with chopped mint, chilli and spring onion, drizzle over a little lime juice and top with the fried shallots and coriander.

SQUID-INK-BATTERED HALIBUT/ THAI GREEN EMULSION

Serves Four

for the emulsion:

6 tbsp fresh coriander
6 tbsp fresh mint leaves
4 Kaffir lime leaves
zest of 1 lemon
4 sticks lemongrass, *crushed, chopped*
1 tbsp fresh ginger, *grated*
1 green chilli, *finely sliced*
15g galangal
400ml sunflower oil
1 egg
1 tbsp lemon juice
1 tbsp white wine vinegar
2 tsp Dijon mustard, *or 1 tsp English mustard powder*
sea salt & black pepper

for the halibut:

1 litre vegetable oil, *for frying*
175g gluten-free self-raising flour
25g squid ink
sea salt & black pepper
4 fillets of halibut, *about 150g each*
400ml sparkling water
75g seasoned plain flour

To make the emulsion, bring a pan of water to the boil, drop in the coriander and mint leaves, blanch for 2 minutes and immediately refresh under cold running water. Drain thoroughly and pat dry on kitchen paper.

Place the Kaffir leaves, lemon zest, lemongrass, grated ginger, chilli, galangal and 100ml sunflower oil into a saucepan and gently heat through. Transfer to a liquidiser together with the coriander and mint and blitz thoroughly. Pass through a fine sieve and set aside to cool.

Place the egg, lemon juice and white wine vinegar into the bowl of a food processor with the mustard and a good seasoning of salt and freshly ground black pepper. Whizz on a high speed and very slowly drizzle in the remaining 300ml of sunflower oil. The mixture will emulsify and then thicken. Remove from the food processor and fold in the cooled liquid, check the seasoning and set aside.

To fry the halibut, heat the oil in a deep fat fryer to 180°C. Mix the self-raising flour and squid ink together in a bowl, season generously with salt and freshly ground pepper, then whisk in enough cold sparkling water to form a runny, lumpy batter, with the consistency of thin cream.

Dip the halibut steaks into the seasoned flour, brushing off any excess and then dip into the batter and again shake off any excess. Carefully lower the coated steaks into the oil and fry for 4 minutes, depending on the thickness of the steaks, until the batter is really crispy.

Remove from the fryer, drain on kitchen paper and serve with the Thai green emulsion.

Spicy seafood

BR
DOVER
HADDOCK/COC
LOBSTER/PL
SEA TROUT
SLIP

*Perfect for any occasion

MAIN COURSES*

POACHED BRILL/ TOMATO HOLLANDAISE

Serves Four

for the stock:
2 medium onions, *peeled, sliced*
1 leek, *chopped*
2 sticks celery, *chopped*
4 carrots, *chopped*
1 whole garlic bulb,
peeled, cut in half
1 handful of fresh herbs, *tarragon,*
parsley, dill, coriander, chervil
275ml white wine
1 tbsp peppercorns
1 lemon, *cut into wedges*
1 small lobe of ginger,
peeled, grated

for the hollandaise:
4 tomatoes
olive oil
sea salt & black pepper
3 egg yolks
½ tsp caster sugar
2 tbsp lemon juice
2 tbsp white wine
1 tbsp white wine vinegar
1 shallot, *peeled, finely sliced*
12 white peppercorns, *cracked*
175g salted butter

for the brill:
1 whole brill, *roughly 1.5kg,*
filleted, with the skin on, 4 fillets
sea salt & black pepper

To make the stock, place the onions, leek, celery, carrots and garlic into a large saucepan, add enough water to just cover and bring to the boil. Simmer for 10 minutes. Take off the heat and add the herbs, wine, peppercorns, lemon and ginger. Return to the heat, and simmer for a further 10 minutes. Turn off and allow the flavours to infuse for 20 minutes. Strain the stock, and allow to cool. The stock will keep in the fridge for up to 5 days, and also freezes well.

To make the hollandaise, preheat the grill to high. Peel, de-seed and chop the tomatoes. Place onto a grill pan, sprinkle over a little olive oil and season with salt and freshly ground black pepper. Grill until the tomatoes just start to char at the edges. Remove from the grill and set aside.

Place the egg yolks, a pinch of salt and the sugar into a food processor. In a small pan heat the lemon juice, wine, vinegar, shallot and peppercorns until the liquid has reduced by half.

In another pan melt the butter and allow it to bubble but not colour. Turn on the food processor and strain in the hot reduced liquor, followed slowly by the hot butter.

Once all the butter has been added, pour the sauce into a bowl and keep it warm, covered with cling film until needed. When ready to serve, stir in the chopped tomatoes.

To poach the brill, when ready to serve, preheat the grill to high. In a pan bring the stock just up to simmering point and carefully lower in the brill. With the stock barely bubbling poach the fish for 5 to 10 minutes (depending on the thickness of the fillets) until the skin just pulls away. Lift the fillets out of the stock and drain.

To serve, carefully peel away the skin from the fillets, lightly season with salt and freshly ground pepper, and put the tomato hollandaise on top of the fish on a grill tray, place under the hot grill for about 2 minutes. Serve immediately with some sautéed potatoes.

Main courses

BRILL POACHED IN RED WINE/ SALSIFY & SEA VEGETABLES

To make the sauce, pour the red wine into a pan with the cinnamon, cloves and citrus zests. Bring to the boil and simmer and reduce by two thirds until a syrupy consistency is reached: add the fish stock, reduce by half again and take off the heat.

Pass through a sieve into another pan, bring to the boil again and reduce by half until the sauce is thick enough to coat the back of a spoon – the sauce should cling to the spoon rather than run off, set aside and keep it warm.

To cook the brill, preheat the oven to 110°C/230°F/gas mark ¼. Clean and wipe the brill. Place the fish into a shallow tray and pour over the red wine sauce, place into the preheated oven and slowly poach for about 10 minutes (cooking time will vary depending on the thickness of the fish: a good way to test is to skewer the fish with a toothpick – if it is cooked the toothpick will go through the fish without resistance). Remove the fish from the pan, set aside and keep it warm.

When the brill is in the oven, bring 500ml of lightly salted water and the butter to the boil, add the salsify and cook until tender: as the water reduces it should add a lovely glaze to the salsify. Add the sea vegetables and boil for 1 minute to finish, and season with salt and freshly ground black pepper.

To serve, garnish the fish with salsify and sea vegetables and spoon over some red wine sauce.

Serves Four

for the sauce:
1 bottle full-bodied red wine, *such as Barolo*
½ cinnamon stick
6 cloves
zest of 1 orange
zest of 1 lemon
500ml brown fish stock, *see page 238*

for the brill:
1 whole brill, roughly 1.5kg, *filleted, skinned*
100g salted butter, *softened*
6 sticks of salsify, *peeled, cut into 5cm batons*
50g mixed sea vegetables, *such as sea asters, sea beets, samphire, sea purslane*
sea salt & black pepper

COD WITH BLACK MISO SAUCE/ SAUTEED LETTUCE & SHALLOT PUREE

Serves Four

for the purée:
900g shallots, *ends trimmed*
120ml olive oil
1 fresh thyme sprig
sea salt & black pepper
1 knob of salted butter
150ml double cream

for the miso sauce:
25g salted butter
1 medium-sized onion, *peeled, sliced*
150g button mushrooms, *sliced*
2 sprigs of thyme
1 tbsp dark miso paste
300g white fish stock, *see page 238*
6 tbsp double cream

for the cod:
4 even-sized cod steaks,
boned, skinned, trimmed
1 knob of salted butter
sea salt & black pepper

for the sautéed lettuce:
rapeseed oil
1 knob of salted butter
2 little gem lettuces, *outer leaves removed, cut into halves*

To make the purée, preheat the oven to 180°C/350°F/gas mark 4. Lay 2 large sheets of foil on top of each other on a work surface. Place the shallots in the centre of the foil, pour over the olive oil, add the thyme and season with salt and freshly ground black pepper. Draw the sides of the foil up to the centre and crinkle the edges to seal and form a parcel. Place on a baking tray and roast in the oven for about 1½ hours until the shallots are really soft. Remove the papery skins and place the shallots in a liquidiser with the butter and cream. Blitz really well and pour into a bowl. Check the seasoning and set aside.

To make the miso sauce, melt the butter in a pan, add the onion, and over a moderate heat cook until softened but not coloured. Add the mushrooms, thyme, miso and fish stock, bring to a simmer and reduce by a third. Add the cream and continue to reduce until the sauce is thick enough to coat the back of a spoon – the sauce should cling to the spoon rather than run off – this will take around 20 minutes. Pass through a sieve into another pan, cover with cling film and set aside until ready to use.

To cook the cod, preheat a water bath to 50°C. Smear the cod steaks with the butter and lightly season with salt and freshly ground black pepper. Place into a vacuum pack bag, and seal loosely. Place the cod steaks into the water bath and cook for 10 minutes.

To sauté the lettuce, at the same time heat a frying pan, add a splash of rapeseed oil and the butter and gently fry the little gem lettuce halves, turning to colour.

To serve, warm the shallot purée and the miso sauce and check the seasoning. Remove the fish from the water bath, snip open the bag and carefully remove. Place the cod steaks on top of the shallot purée and the lettuce. Spoon over some hot miso sauce and serve immediately.

Main courses

 196 — 197

CRAB LASAGNE

Serves Four

for the pasta:
500g '00' pasta flour
8 eggs, *use 3 whole eggs,*
lightly whisked with 5 egg yolks
2 tbsp olive oil
1 pinch of saffron,
infused in 1 tbsp boiling water

for the sauce:
1 shallot, *peeled, finely sliced*
1 tbsp olive oil
1 strip of lemon peel
25ml Noilly Prat vermouth
120ml whipping cream
50g Gruyère cheese, *grated*

for the lasagne:
200g fresh white crab meat
4 plum tomatoes, *skinned*
sea salt & black pepper
olive oil
rapeseed oil
150g baby spinach

To make the pasta, place all the ingredients into a food processor and pulse to bring together. Turn out onto a lightly floured work surface and knead well. Divide into 4, wrap in cling film and refrigerate to rest for 2 hours.

Cut each piece of dough into 2. Take 1 of the pieces and, on a lightly floured surface, flatten with your hands. Roll the dough through a pasta machine repeatedly, gradually making your way to 2 notches from the thinnest setting. Lay the resulting long strip of pasta on your work surface. Using a 7.5cm round cutter, cut out discs. Repeat with the other piece of pasta dough. You need 2 discs per serving for the lasagne, although I always cut a couple of extra. Allow the pasta discs to dry out while you make the Gruyère cream sauce.

To make the sauce, fry the shallot in the olive oil until softened, add the lemon peel and vermouth and bring to the boil. Simmer to reduce the liquid by half. Add the cream and Gruyère, bring back to the boil and simmer again. Pass through a sieve into another saucepan and set aside.

To make the lasagne, pick over the crab meat to remove any pieces of shell, slice the tomatoes, set aside. Drop the pasta discs into a pan of gently boiling salted water. Cook for about 3 minutes, then lift out with a slotted spoon. Quickly season with salt and freshly ground black pepper and add a splash of olive oil. Meanwhile, heat a frying pan, add a splash of rapeseed oil and sauté the spinach until just wilted and season with salt and freshly ground black pepper.

Preheat the oven to 200°C/400°F/gas mark 6. Lightly oil a large baking tray and lay on 4 pasta discs. Divide the spinach between the discs and top with the white crab meat and 2 slices of tomato. Finish with another pasta disc and spoon over the Gruyère sauce. Place in the oven and bake for 10 to 15 minutes, until bubbling and lightly browned. Serve immediately.

DOVER SOLE/ CAFE DE PARIS BUTTER

Serves Four

for the Café de Paris butter:
35g tomato ketchup
25g English mustard
25g capers
2 shallots, *peeled, finely sliced*
1 handful parsley, *finely chopped*
1 tbsp chives, *snipped*
$\frac{1}{2}$ tsp marjoram, *finely chopped*
$\frac{1}{2}$ tsp thyme leaves
6 tarragon leaves, *finely chopped*
$\frac{1}{2}$ tsp rosemary, *finely chopped*
1 garlic clove, *peeled, finely sliced*
6 anchovy fillets, *finely chopped*
1 tbsp brandy
1 tbsp Madeira
$\frac{1}{2}$ tsp Worcestershire sauce
1 tbsp paprika
$\frac{1}{2}$ tsp curry powder
$\frac{1}{2}$ tsp cayenne
1 lemon, zest and juice
1 orange, *zest only*
1 tsp salt
300g salted butter, *at room temperature, cut into small cubes*

for the Dover sole:
rapeseed oil
1 knob of salted butter
4 whole Dover sole, *1 per portion, cleaned, skinned, head removed*

To make the Café de Paris butter, combine all the ingredients except the butter in a large bowl, set aside. Beat the butter until fluffy, then mix with the other ingredients. Transfer to a sheet of cling film and shape into a neat log about 2.5cm in diameter. Wrap in the cling film and refrigerate for at least 1 hour to firm up. This will make more butter than you need for this recipe, but it can be kept in the freezer for up to 3 months: it's good on steaks, chicken and fish.

To fry the Dover sole, preheat the grill to high. Heat a frying pan over a moderate heat, add a splash of rapeseed oil and the butter. Add the fish and fry for approximately 3 minutes on each side to achieve a golden colour. The fish is ready when the flesh in the centre 'gives' a little when pressed with your thumb.

Just before removing the fish from the pan cut circles of the Café de Paris butter and place 3 along the length of each fish. Flash under the grill to melt the butter: by the time the fish reaches the table the butter should be melting all over the fish.

Serve immediately with a tossed green salad and buttered new potatoes.

GALTON'S FISH PIE

Serves Four

for the topping:
900g Maris Piper potatoes,
peeled weight, chunkily chopped
150g salted butter
6 tbsp milk
4 tbsp double cream
3 egg yolks
sea salt & black pepper

for the fish pie:
300g undyed smoked haddock,
kept whole and with skin on
560ml milk
1 sprig of rosemary
1 medium onion, *peeled, sliced*
rapeseed oil
12 king scallops
225g salmon fillet, *skinned,*
cubed evenly into 3cm cubes
225g cod fillet, *skinned,*
cubed evenly into 3cm cubes
170g cooked peeled prawns
140g salted butter
110g plain flour
400ml whipping cream
3 hard-boiled eggs, *chopped*
3 tbsp mini capers, *drained,*
rinsed of brine
4 tbsp chopped parsley
2 tbsp lemon juice
sea salt & black pepper

There are fish pies, and there are fish pies: this one is a real winner made with plenty of chunky fresh fish, and a potato topping, rather than pastry. It is important that the fish is 'barely cooked' before making the pie to give it plenty of texture and bite.

To make the topping, place the potatoes into a saucepan of cold salted water, bring to the boil and cook until very soft. Drain, and leave in the colander to extract as much liquid as possible. Push the warm potatoes through a ricer into a bowl and then beat in the butter, milk, cream and egg yolks. Season with salt and freshly ground black pepper and set aside.

To make the fish pie: place the haddock into a shallow saucepan together with the milk, rosemary and onion, and poach it over a moderate heat for about 5 minutes. Remove the poached haddock from the milk with a slotted spoon and set aside. Strain the milk and set aside. When cool enough to handle, remove the skin from the haddock and flake chunkily.

Heat a frying pan over a high heat, add a splash of rapeseed oil and very quickly sear the scallops on each side – just enough to colour them.

Arrange all the fish, including the prawns, in the bottom of an ovenproof dish, roughly 30 x 22cm.

Melt the butter in a saucepan and add the flour. Cook over a medium heat for a couple of minutes and pour in the strained milk, and with the pan still on the heat beat continuously until you have a thick béchamel-type sauce. Add the cream and heat again, stirring continuously. Remove from the heat and then carefully stir in the chopped eggs, capers, parsley and lemon juice and season with salt and freshly ground black pepper. Pour this mixture over the fish.

Preheat the oven to 180°C/350°F/gas mark 4. Place the fish into the oven for 20 minutes until it is heated through.

About 10 minutes before serving preheat the grill to high. Reheat the potatoes in a saucepan over a moderate heat and spread the topping over the fish. Place the fish pie under the grill for a couple of minutes to colour the potatoes. Serve immediately.

ROAST HALIBUT/ BRIOCHE & HERB BUTTER CRUST

To make the herb butter, strip the leaves from the parsley, chop roughly and place into the bowl of a food processor and whizz well. Add the softened butter and drained capers. Gently roast the fennel seeds in a dry frying pan until lightly coloured (this helps to enhance the flavour) and place these in the food processor with the snipped chives and a good seasoning of salt and freshly ground pepper, and whizz again until everything is well combined. Lay a piece of greaseproof paper onto your work surface and scrape the mixture out of the food processor onto it. Place another piece of greaseproof paper on top and using a rolling pin roll out thinly. Place onto a tray and into the fridge for 2 hours to firm up.

To roast the halibut and brioche, preheat the oven to 180°C/350°F/gas mark 4 and preheat the grill to high. Slice the brioche very thinly and cut out rectangular shapes the size of each halibut fillet. At the same time remove the herb butter from the fridge and cut out rectangular shapes to the same size, and return to the fridge. (Any leftover butter can be frozen for up to 1 month and used for another dish.)

Paint each piece of brioche on both sides with melted butter and place on top of the halibut fillets. Place these onto a baking tray and into the preheated oven for 5 minutes.

Remove from the oven and lay a piece of herb butter on top of each piece of brioche. Grill for about 30 seconds until the butter is bubbling and turning lightly brown, serve immediately.

Serves Four

for the herb butter:
1 good bunch of flat leaf parsley
200g salted butter, *softened*
1 heaped tsp capers, *rinsed, drained*
$1/2$ tsp fennel seeds
1 small bunch of chives, *snipped*
sea salt & black pepper

for the halibut and brioche:
1 small brioche loaf
75g melted butter
4 fillets of halibut,
roughly 150g each on the bone

"OVER THE LAST 30 YE
WE EAT AND HOW WE
BEYOND ALL RECOGNIT
YOU'D ONLY EVER SEE
AN ENGLISH MENU —
HADDOCK. NOW THERE
THAT WE CAN'T GET EN

ARS THE FOOD THAT
EAT IT HAS CHANGED
ON. IN THE EIGHTIES
A COUPLE OF FISH ON
USUALLY COD AND
S SO MUCH CHOICE
UGH OF IT"

Main courses

HADDOCK, COCKLE & PRAWN CHOWDER

Serves Four

300g cockles
50g flour
rapeseed oil
2 large shallots, *peeled, finely sliced*
4 garlic cloves, *peeled, grated*
175ml dry white wine
1 large white onion, *peeled, sliced*
425ml white fish stock,
see page 238
100g boiled small new potatoes
1 pinch of saffron
1 large red chilli, *finely sliced*
250ml whipping cream
50g petit pois
100g fresh sweetcorn kernels,
grilled to colour, taken off the cob
300g undyed smoked haddock,
cubed in 2cm dice
300g prawns, *cooked, shells off*
lime juice to taste
sea salt & black pepper
4 tbsp chopped coriander

Place the cockles in their shells into a bowl and cover with cold slightly salted water, sprinkle some flour over the top, refrigerate and leave overnight, or at least for a couple of hours (ingesting this flour will encourage the cockles to spit out any sand and grit).

Drain the cockles in a colander then leave under cold, running water for a few minutes to get rid of the flour. Heat a good splash of rapeseed oil in a large pan over a medium heat, add the shallots and 2 of the garlic cloves, and fry until just starting to colour. Turn up the heat and, when the pan is really hot, tip the cockles in and give them a good shake. Add the white wine, cover and cook over a high heat for a few minutes until the cockles have opened, then take off the heat and set aside.

Once the cockles are cool enough to handle, remove them from the shells and set them aside in a bowl, discarding any that have not opened. Strain the cooking liquor through a muslin cloth into a large bowl and reserve.

Heat 4 tablespoons of rapeseed oil in a large frying pan and gently fry the onion and remaining 2 cloves of garlic until softened and just beginning to brown. Add the stock and the potatoes, bring to the boil and simmer for a few minutes. Next add the saffron, chillies and cream and continue to simmer to reduce a little.

Finally add the peas, sweetcorn and haddock, followed by the cockles and prawns. Season with lime juice, salt and freshly ground pepper, and just before serving stir in the chopped coriander.

OPEN LOBSTER PIE

Serves Four

for the pastry:
250g plain flour
1 tsp salt
1 tsp sugar
150g salted butter, *softened*
1 egg, beaten

for the pie:
3 whole eggs plus 2 egg yolks,
lightly whisked together
425ml double cream
100g grated Cheddar cheese
1 pinch of freshly grated nutmeg
sea salt & black pepper
3 cooked lobsters,
just the meat, chunkily chopped
4 tbsp chopped basil

For this recipe you'll need 4 individual 7.5cm loose-bottomed flan rings, at least 4cm high, and some baking beans.

To make the pastry, sift the flour onto a large clean work surface and sprinkle over the salt and sugar. Make a well in the centre and add the softened butter along with the beaten egg. Using your fingertips amalgamate the butter and egg until you achieve a scrambled egg consistency then add a good splash of water and mix in. Draw in the flour and again using your fingertips bring the pastry together. Wrap in cling film and refrigerate to rest for at least 1 hour.

When ready to use, remove the pastry from the fridge, roll out, and line the flan rings. Place on a baking tray and return to the fridge to rest for at least another 1 hour.

To make the pie, preheat the oven to 160°C/325°F/gas mark 3. Remove the lined flan rings from the fridge, cover the pastry-lined rings with baking parchment, fill with baking beans and place in the centre of the oven. Bake 'blind' for about 25 minutes, or until the pastry just starts to colour. Remove the baking beans and parchment: if there are any cracks in the pastry, use leftover pieces of pastry or beaten egg yolk to repair it. Return the pastry case to the oven for about 5 minutes, remove from the oven and leave to cool.

Whisk the eggs, egg yolks and cream together in a bowl. Add the cheese and season well with grated nutmeg, salt and freshly ground pepper. Add the lobster and chopped basil and mix well.

Spoon the lobster mixture into the pastry cases and bake in the preheated oven for 40 minutes or until the tarts are set. Take out of the oven and allow to rest for 10 minutes before serving.

To serve, trim the pastry and remove the flan rings, and serve with a light tomato and cucumber salad and some blanched asparagus.

Main courses

For this recipe you'll need to kill the lobsters and remove the tails and claws. The most humane way to do this is to quickly insert the point of a sharp knife in its head where the cross is.

To make the pasta, place all the pasta ingredients into a food processor and pulse to bring together. Turn out onto a lightly floured work surface and knead well. Divide into 4, wrap in cling film and refrigerate to rest for 2 hours.

To make the ravioli, bring a pan of salted water to the boil and drop in the lobster claws to cook for 5 minutes. After 2 minutes add the tails, simmer for 3 minutes, remove immediately and refresh in iced water. Remove the shells from the lobster meat and chop the meat into small chunks. Cover and refrigerate until needed.

Place the salmon and egg into a food processor, season with salt and freshly ground pepper and blitz well. Pass through a sieve into a bowl. Fold in the cream, parsley, lemon juice and lobster. Cover and refrigerate to firm up for 1 hour. When it has firmed up, form it into 30g balls, place onto a greaseproof-covered tray, cover with cling film and return to the fridge.

Roll a piece of the pasta dough through a pasta machine repeatedly, gradually making your way to the finest setting. Once this has been reached, cut the sheet of pasta in half, and get a pot of water and a pastry brush ready – work quickly to prevent the pasta from drying out.

Lay the sheet of the pasta on the work surface and place the balls of lobster meat onto the pasta about 6cm apart and brush water around. Tightly press the second sheet of pasta on top, pressing down round the balls of lobster, cut out with a round pastry cutter, and press or crimp round the edges of the pasta rings to ensure there is no air inside. Repeat this with another piece of pasta dough until all of the filling is used up.

To serve, bring a pan of salted water to a gentle simmer, drop in the ravioli and cook for 5 minutes. Using a slotted spoon lift them out of the water and place on kitchen paper to drain. At the same time heat the bisque until hot.

Place the ravioli into a bowl and spoon over the bisque, scatter over the ham and melon and garnish with cornflower and sorrel leaves.

LOBSTER RAVIOLI/ SHELLFISH BISQUE

Serves Four

for the pasta:
500g '00' pasta flour
8 eggs, *lightly whisk*
3 whole eggs with 5 egg yolks
2 tbsp olive oil
1 pinch of saffron,
infused in 1 tbsp boiling water

for the ravioli:
2 live lobsters
200g salmon fillet, *diced*
1 egg
sea salt & black pepper
200g double cream
1 tbsp parsley, *chopped*
juice of half a lemon
250ml shellfish bisque,
see page 240
1 really ripe Charentais melon,
peeled, sliced into thin strips
100g Iberico ham,
torn into thin strips
1 handful of cornflowers
1 handful of buckler sorrel

LOBSTER/ ZUCCHINI FRIES

Serves Four

for the lobster:
4 live lobsters
olive oil
salted butter
sea salt & black pepper
1 lemon, *cut into wedges*

for the zucchini fries:
6 zucchini *(aka courgettes)*
sea salt & black pepper
1 litre vegetable oil, *for frying*
100g seasoned flour
1 tsp smoked paprika
2 eggs and 100ml milk,
beaten together to make an egg wash

For this recipe you'll need to kill the lobsters and remove the tails and claws. The most humane way to do this is to quickly insert the point of a sharp knife in its head where the cross is.

To cook the lobsters, bring a pan of salted water to the boil and drop in the lobster claws to cook for 5 minutes. After 2 minutes add the tails, simmer for 3 minutes, remove immediately and refresh in iced water. Remove the shells from the lobster meat and chop the meat into small chunks and set aside.

To make the zucchini fries, cut the zucchini into large matchsticks, leaving the skin on, and lay on kitchen paper and sprinkle with a teaspoon of salt. Refrigerate for half an hour to extract the moisture, and then wash, drain and pat them dry.

Use two separate bowls: place the seasoned flour into one and mix it with the smoked paprika, and the egg wash into another.

Heat the vegetable oil in a deep fat fryer to 180°C. Quickly dip the zucchini into the egg wash, shaking off any excess as you lift them out, and then lightly dust in the flour.

Drop the zucchini into the fryer and fry until golden brown. Remove from the oil and drain on kitchen paper, season with flakes of sea salt and keep them warm.

Heat a large frying pan, add some olive oil and a knob of butter. When the butter starts to foam add the lobster and fry, turning as you do so until lightly coloured and cooked through, season with salt and freshly ground pepper.

Serve the lobster with the zucchini fries and wedges of fresh lemon.

Main courses

T-BONE PLAICE WITH BABY SQUID/ CHAMPAGNE & CAVIAR SAUCE

To make the sauce, melt 50g of the butter in a saucepan over a medium heat, add the shallot, carrot and mushrooms and sweat until just softened but not coloured. Add half of the champagne and reduce by a third to a syrupy consistency. Next add the white fish stock and reduce by half, and finally add the cream and simmer, and once again reduce by half.

Pass through a sieve into a clean saucepan and then over a low heat whisk in the remaining butter and season with salt and freshly ground pepper. Set aside until ready to use.

To fry the plaice and squid, remove the head from the plaice and with a sharp knife cut lengthways through the bone straight down the centre line of the fish to give 2 fillets on the bone, cut into 4 steaks and set aside.

Clean and wash the squid, pat dry, cut off the tentacles, slice the body into rings and set aside.

Heat a frying pan over a medium heat, add a splash of oil and the butter. When the butter starts to foam, add the plaice steaks, fry for 3 to 4 minutes on each side to achieve a deep brown colour on the dark skin side and a golden colour on the lighter skin side, season with salt and freshly ground pepper.

At the same time reheat the sauce until hot, and stir in the remaining champagne, add the caviar and check the seasoning.

Heat another pan on a high heat, add a good splash of oil, throw in the squid and fry for a couple of minutes, season with salt and freshly ground pepper.

Serve the plaice and fried squid with the champagne and caviar sauce over the top. Garnish with sea beet leaves and serve with some wilted spinach.

Serves Four

for the sauce:
200g salted butter
1 large shallot, *peeled, finely sliced*
1 medium carrot, *peeled, finely sliced*
6 button mushrooms, *sliced*
200ml champagne
300ml white fish stock, *see page 238*
300ml double cream
sea salt & black pepper
1 tbsp Sevruga caviar

for the plaice and squid:
1 large plaice, *roughly 1.5kg*
400g baby squid
rapeseed oil
1 knob of salted butter
sea salt & black pepper
1 handful of sea beet leaves

SALT-CRUSTED SEA BASS/ CITRUS BUTTER SAUCE

Serves Four

for the sauce:
2 oranges
2 shallots, *peeled, finely sliced*
1 tbsp white wine vinegar
4 tbsp white wine
225g salted butter, *cut into cubes*

for the sea bass:
1 whole wild sea bass, *roughly 1kg, gutted, gills removed, scaled, trimmed*
100g egg whites
500g fine table salt
juice and rind of 2 lemons

To make the sauce, squeeze the juice from 1 orange, place into a saucepan over a medium heat and bring to a simmer, reduce by half. Grate the zest of the second orange onto a plate and set aside, then peel the orange and segment it, chop the segments and set aside.

Place the finely sliced shallots, reduced orange juice, wine vinegar, and white wine into a pan. Bring to the boil and reduce the liquid until you have about 2 tablespoons. Add 1 tablespoon of cold water and reduce again until you have 1 tablespoon of liquid.

Turn the heat down and whisk in the butter, about 25g at a time. The sauce will emulsify. Once all the butter has been added, remove the pan from the heat, then pass through a sieve into another saucepan. Set aside until needed, but do not refrigerate or the sauce will separate.

To bake the sea bass, begin by cutting out a fish-shaped piece of thick cardboard, about 2cm larger than the sea bass which you are going to cook. Cover with 2 layers of tin foil, place onto a baking tray and lay the whole fish on top.

Place the egg whites into the bowl of an electric food mixer and whisk on high speed to soft peaks. Add the salt slowly along with the lemon juice and rind and continue to whisk until the egg whites are firm and smooth like a meringue. Using a palette knife, spread the mixture evenly over the whole fish, taking it right down to the foil to make an airtight seal.

Preheat the oven to 200°C/400°F/gas mark 6. Carefully place into the preheated oven and bake for 25 minutes until the crust is golden, then insert a cake tester into the thickest part of the fish for 10 seconds to check if it is cooked. The tester should feel just hot: if it is only lukewarm the fish needs to cook for a little longer. Once cooked, the fish will 'hold' without spoiling under the crust for about 10 minutes.

At the same time reheat the sauce until hot, stirring continuously, and add the orange zest and chopped segments.

To serve, transfer the salt-crusted fish to a large chopping board. Break the crust open with a knife, remove the fish and carefully fillet, making sure you remove all of the bones, and serve with the citrus butter sauce.

Main courses

GRILLED SEA BASS/
CHAMPAGNE & SHRIMP SAUCE

To make the sauce, melt 50g of the butter in a saucepan over a medium heat, add the shallot, carrot and mushrooms and sweat until just softened but not coloured. Add half of the champagne and reduce by a third to a syrupy consistency. Next add the white fish stock and reduce by half, and finally add the cream and simmer, and once again reduce by half.

Pass through a sieve into a clean saucepan and then over a low heat whisk in the remaining butter and season with salt and freshly ground pepper. Set aside until ready to use.

To cook the leeks and mushrooms, bring a pan of salted water to the boil, drop in the leeks and blanch for a couple of minutes. Drain thoroughly and set aside. Heat a frying pan, add the butter and sauté the mushrooms. Add the leeks and make sure they are heated through, add a little more butter if necessary, and keep them warm.

To grill the sea bass, preheat the grill to high. Score the skin of the sea bass fillets, being careful not to cut too deeply into the flesh. Season the flesh side of the fish with salt and freshly ground pepper, then arrange, skin side up, on a well-buttered tray. Brush the scored skin with olive oil, and place the fillets under the preheated grill. Cook for approximately 4 minutes or until the skin has blackened and the flesh is just cooked.

At the same time reheat the sauce until hot, and stir in the remaining champagne and add the brown shrimps, and check the seasoning.

Serve the leeks and mushrooms and the grilled sea bass with the champagne sauce over the top.

Serves Four

for the sauce:
200g salted butter
1 shallot, *peeled, finely sliced*
1 medium carrot,
peeled, finely sliced
6 button mushrooms, *sliced*
200ml champagne
300ml white fish stock,
see page 238
300ml double cream
sea salt & black pepper
150g peeled brown shrimps

for the leeks and mushrooms:
1 leek, trimmed, *cut in half lengthways, finely sliced*
150g black trompette mushrooms, *or any other wild mushrooms, cleaned*
1 knob of salted butter

for the sea bass:
700-900g sea bass, *descaled, pin bones removed, cut into 4 fillets*
sea salt & black pepper
olive oil

SEA TROUT BALLOTINE/ TOMATO CONSOMME & ROASTED TOMATOES

Serves Four

for the consommé:
500g ripe cherry vine tomatoes, *off the stalk, halved*
2 shallots, *peeled, finely sliced*
25ml olive oil
1 tbsp caster sugar
20g fresh basil
sea salt & black pepper

for the roasted tomatoes:
12 cherry vine tomatoes
sea salt & black pepper
rapeseed oil

for the ballotine:
1 side of sea trout, *roughly 400g*
12 tbsp finely chopped mixed herbs, *chervil, parsley, mint, chives*
20g salt
grated zest of 1 lemon
1 sprig tarragon
1 handful of marigold petals
basil oil, *see page 236*

To make the consommé, place all the ingredients in the bowl of a food processor. Season really well with salt and freshly ground black pepper (this helps to extract the juices from the tomatoes), then whizz on a high speed. Once it is really well processed, pour into a jelly bag or a large piece of muslin suspended over a bowl. Tie up securely and leave for 4 hours in a cool place, or until all the juices have dripped through. Chill the consommé until needed.

To roast the tomatoes, heat the oven to 100°C/210°F/gas mark ¼. Place the tomatoes onto a baking tray, season with salt and freshly ground black pepper and drizzle with a good helping of rapeseed oil. Place in the oven for 1¼ hours – the tomatoes will shrivel slightly and the flavour will intensify. Remove from the oven and set aside to cool.

To make the ballotine, carefully skin the sea trout and cut in half lengthways. Take one half and turn it completely: the head side from one half should now be touching the tail side from the other half.

Mix the chopped herbs, salt and lemon zest together in a tray and roll both halves of the sea trout in the herb mixture. Place one half of the fish on top of the other (you should have an even shape) and roll very tightly in cling film, tying each end as tight as possible to form a ballotine.

Fill a deep-sided roasting tray to two thirds of its depth with warm water and heat on the stove to bring the temperature up to 50°C. Lower the cling-film-wrapped ballotine into the water and cook for 1 hour, using a thermometer to maintain the water temperature at 50°C (or use a water bath). Chill immediately in iced water and then refrigerate for at least 2 hours to firm up.

To serve, slice the ballotine into 4 pieces – the slices should be about 6cm thick. Pour the chilled consommé around the ballotine and add roast tomatoes, tarragon leaves, marigold petals and add a splash of basil oil.

Main courses

FILLET OF SEA TROUT/ SAMPHIRE & BEURRE BLANC

To make the beurre blanc, place the shallots into a saucepan together with the wine vinegar, lemon juice and white wine. Bring to the boil and reduce the liquid to about a tablespoon. Add 1 tablespoon of cold water, and keep on the heat to reduce the liquid again to just a tablespoon.

Turn the heat down and over a low heat, whisk in the butter about 25g at a time. The sauce will emulsify. Once all the butter has been added, remove the pan from the heat and pass the sauce through a sieve into another saucepan. Set aside until needed, but do not refrigerate or the sauce will separate.

Serves Four

for the beurre blanc:
2 shallots, *peeled, finely sliced*
1 tbsp wine vinegar
2 tbsp lemon juice
4 tbsp white wine
225g salted butter, *cubed*
zest of half 1 lemon, *finely grated*
sea salt & black pepper

To cook the sea trout, heat a frying pan over a medium heat, add a good splash of rapeseed oil and the butter. When the butter foams place the fillets in the pan, season, press down firmly on the fillets and fry for 3 to 4 minutes. Turn the fish over and fry for a further 30 seconds, again seasoning with salt and freshly ground black pepper as you do so.

for the sea trout:
4 x 150g fillets of sea trout,
skinned, pin bones removed
rapeseed oil
1 knob of salted butter
sea salt & black pepper

To cook the samphire, bring a pan of unsalted water to the boil, throw in the samphire and cook for 3 minutes. Drain thoroughly, smother with butter and season with salt and freshly ground black pepper.

for the samphire:
250g samphire, *carefully picked over and washed thoroughly*
25g salted butter
sea salt & black pepper

Just before serving reheat the beurre blanc, carefully stirring the sauce over a low heat, stir in the lemon zest and check the seasoning.

Serve the sea trout on a bed of buttered samphire with the lemon beurre blanc.

SKATE WINGS/
BUERRE
NOISETTE

To make the beurre noisette, melt the butter in a saucepan over a medium heat, continue cooking until it starts to turn golden. You are aiming for caramel-coloured granules in the butter – when that stage is reached, add the lemon juice, simmer for 2 minutes and set aside.

To cook the skate wings, preheat the oven to 200°C/400°F/gas mark 6. Heat a frying pan until hot, then add the oil and butter. Once the butter is foaming, add the skate wings – you may need to do this one at a time if your pan isn't big enough – and fry until coloured on both sides (really fresh wings may start to shrink and curl, but this is normal).

Serves Four

for the beurre noisette:
110g salted butter
juice of 1 large lemon
2 tbsp very small capers
3 tbsp chopped parsley

for the skate wings:
2 tbsp rapeseed oil
25g salted butter
4 whole skate wings
sea salt & black pepper

Remove the skate wings from the pan and place on a baking tray. Season with salt and freshly ground black pepper and place in the oven for about 5 minutes, depending on how thick the wings are (the fish is cooked when it just starts to come apart when pressed).

To serve, warm the beurre noisette, and add the capers and chopped parsley, and spoon it over the skate wings, making sure each portion has plenty of capers.

Main courses

SLIP SOLE/
PAPRIKA
BUTTER

To make the paprika butter, combine all the ingredients in a bowl. Form into a sausage shape and wrap tightly in cling film. Refrigerate for at least 1 hour to firm up.

To cook the slip sole, preheat the oven to 200°C/400°F/gas mark 6. Using a sharp pair of scissors, take the head and tail off and trim the perimeter of the fish. Heat a frying pan until it starts to smoke. Coat the fish in a little olive oil and place in the pan. Don't turn it too soon, otherwise the fish might stick. Repeat on the other side until the fish is well marked. Remove from the pan and place on a metal tray. Lightly season with salt and freshly ground black pepper and finish in the oven for about 3 minutes, just until the fish starts to come away from the bone.

To serve, thinly slice the paprika butter and arrange 3 slices in a row on top of each fish. Allow to melt a little, and then serve with chips and a dressed salad.

Serves Four

for the paprika butter:
200g unsalted butter, *softened*
1 tbsp super fine capers
1 tbsp smoked paprika
juice of ½ lemon
2 tbsp chopped parsley
50g peeled brown shrimps
sea salt & black pepper

for the slip sole:
4 slip soles, *roughly 250g each, skins taken off both sides, but kept whole*
olive oil
sea salt & black pepper

ROAST TURBOT/ LEMON EMULSION WITH PANCETTA & LEEKS

Serves Four

for the turbot:

1 whole wild turbot, *roughly 2.5kg*
1 leek
2 fennel bulbs
2 sticks of celery
1 large white onion
1 lemon
1 good handful each of parsley stalks, chervil and thyme
1 bottle of champagne, *or sparkling wine*
1 handful of sea aster leaves
1 handful of oyster leaves, *optional*

for the emulsion:

110g salted butter
juice of 1 large lemon
1 tbsp champagne vinegar
sea salt & black pepper

for the pancetta and leeks:

2 leeks, white part only, *finely sliced*
100g salted butter
60g pancetta lardons
1 garlic clove, *peeled, grated*
sea salt & black pepper

To roast the turbot, unless you're confident about doing it yourself ask your fishmonger to prepare the fish for you. Remove the head, clean the fish thoroughly making sure there is no roe left inside, and keep the fish whole.

Preheat the oven to 180°C/350°F/gas mark 4. Finely slice all the vegetables and lemon and spread on a roasting tray, strew the herbs over the vegetables and lay the fish on top. Pour the champagne over the fish and place in the preheated oven to cook for 30 minutes. Test with a food probe, the thickest part of the fish should read 42°C. The fish will start to come away from the bone and the skin will peel back very easily when it is cooked. Lift the fish out of the roasting tray and set aside somewhere warm to rest.

To make the emulsion, melt the butter in a saucepan over a medium heat, continue cooking until it starts to turn golden. You are aiming for caramel-coloured granules in the butter – when that stage is reached, add the lemon juice, simmer for 2 minutes and set aside.

Pass the cooking liquor from the turbot through a sieve into a saucepan. Over a moderate heat bring it to the boil and simmer to reduce by half. Slowly whisk in the lemon and butter, season with champagne vinegar, salt and freshly ground pepper, and keep it warm.

To cook the pancetta and leeks, blanch the leeks in boiling water for 1 minute, then immediately refresh under cold running water and drain thoroughly. Melt the butter in a large pan over a medium heat and when foaming add the pancetta and fry until crispy. Add the garlic and leeks and cook in the butter. Season with salt and freshly ground pepper.

To serve, carefully remove the skin from the fish (it should peel off easily when cooked). Lift 4 portions of turbot from the bone and serve with the buttered leeks, crispy pancetta and lemon emulsion. Garnish with sea aster and oyster leaves.

BAS

STO

STOCK/WH

LANGO

SHE

*Oil, stocks and bisque

THE BASICS*

BASIL OIL

Makes roughly 150ml

3 large bunches of basil, *leaves only*
150ml olive oil
sea salt & black pepper

To make the oil, heat a pan of salted water until boiling then add the basil leaves. Blanch for 20 seconds only, then refresh immediately under cold running water.

Pat the leaves dry, place in a food processor with the oil and blitz on a high speed for a few minutes until the oil turns a vibrant green.

Push through a sieve into a bowl. Season with salt and freshly ground black pepper, and refrigerate, tightly covered with cling film until required.

The oil can be stored in the fridge for up to 2 weeks, or frozen.

CHICKEN STOCK

Makes roughly 3 litres

1 large onion, *peeled and chopped*
1 large carrot, *peeled and chopped*
1 stalk of celery, *chopped*
½ bulb of fennel, *chopped*
2 cloves of garlic, *peeled and crushed*
vegetable oil
1kg uncooked chicken bones
250ml white wine
a few sprigs of parsley, tarragon, dill and chervil

To make the stock, in a large saucepan gently fry the onion, carrot, celery, fennel and garlic in a splash of vegetable oil until they start to soften but not colour.

Add the chicken bones, wine and herbs and at least 5 litres of water to cover. Bring to the boil, and skim off any scum that forms on the top. Turn the heat down and simmer very gently for a maximum of 3 hours.

Strain through a fine sieve. The stock is now ready to use. Allow to cool and refrigerate, it can be stored in the fridge for up to 4 days, or frozen for up to 2 months.

If you prefer a stronger flavour, return the stock to the heat and boil to reduce until you have the desired intensity of flavour. At Morston, I keep this stock light, as it's the backbone of many of our soups and risottos, and I prefer not to have too strong a chicken flavour coming through.

BASIL OIL —

Spicy fish soup, grilled red mullet & rouille — 154

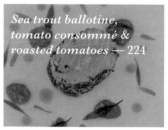

Sea trout ballotine, tomato consommé & roasted tomatoes — 224

CHICKEN STOCK —

Smoked haddock, pea & lime soup, chive oil — 38

Oyster crackers — 92

Tiger prawn & haricot bean soup, curry oil — 98

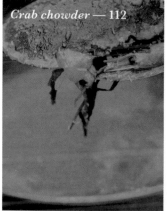

Crab chowder — 112

Crab & potato 'risotto' — 114

Brown shrimp risotto — 148

Spiced monkfish, saffron rice — 158

Tiger prawn & noodle broth — 170

Fruity seafood curry — 176

Squid in black bean sauce, deep-fried shallots — 186

BROWN FISH STOCK

Makes roughly 2 litres

1.3kg white fish bones, *such as plaice, sole or brill*
olive oil
250ml white wine
250g onions, *peeled and chopped*
2 cloves garlic, *peeled and sliced*
300g button mushrooms, *chopped*
250g carrots, *peeled and chopped*
a good handful of parsley stalks
2 star anise
2 litres white fish stock, *see opposite*

To make the stock, preheat the oven to 200°C/400°F/gas mark 6. Lay the fish in a large roasting tray, splash over a little olive oil and roast the bones until dark brown all over. Remove from the oven, take the fish from the tray and place in a large saucepan.

Deglaze the roasting tray with the white wine, scraping all the bits off you can and add this to the bones.

In another pan heat 6 tablespoons of olive oil, add the onion and sauté until browned, then add the garlic, mushrooms and carrots and sauté. Add the parsley stalks and star anise. Once everything is lightly coloured add this to the fish bones.

Now cover the bones in the fish stock. Bring up to simmering point and simmer for up to 1 hour, and then strain the liquid through a fine sieve.

The stock is now ready to use. Allow to cool and refrigerate. It can be stored in the fridge for up to 4 days, or frozen for up to 2 months.

The stock is great for soups and curries, and can be reduced by half to intensify the flavour, and reduced further again to use as a fish sauce.

WHITE FISH STOCK

Makes roughly 2 litres

1 onion, *peeled and chopped*
1 bulb of fennel, *chopped*
1 leek, *chopped*
2 sticks of celery, *chopped*
10g unsalted butter
1.3kg white fish bones, *such as turbot, halibut or sole*
275ml white wine
1 bouquet garni, *made up of parsley, tarragon and dill*
1 lemon, *cut into wedges*

To make the stock, gently sweat the onion, fennel, leek and celery in the butter in a large saucepan until they are soft but not browned. Add the fish bones and white wine. Top up with 1.7 litres of cold water and bring gently to the boil, skimming off any scum that rises to the surface. Add the bouquet garni and the lemon wedges and then simmer gently for 20 minutes, and then strain the liquid through a fine sieve.

The stock is now ready to use. Allow to cool and refrigerate. It can be stored in the fridge for up to 4 days, or frozen for up to 2 months.

This stock is a sound base for fish soups, fish risottos and fish sauces.

The basics

BROWN FISH STOCK —

Spicy fish soup, grilled red mullet & rouille — 154

Brill poached in red wine, salsify & sea vegetables — 194

WHITE FISH STOCK —

Lobster curry — 44

Blow-torched sea bream, sauternes & curry sauce — 62

Pan-fried scallops, roasted vegetables & Nantua sauce — 138

Spicy fish soup, grilled red mullet & rouille — 154

Tiger prawn & potato curry, samphire & broad beans — 168

Roasted scallops, Sauternes & curry sauce with cauliflower — 180

Cod with black miso sauce, sautéed lettuce & shallot purée — 196

Haddock, cockle & prawn chowder — 210

T-bone plaice with baby squid, champagne & caviar sauce — 218

Grilled sea bass, champagne & shrimp sauce — 222

LANGOUSTINE STOCK

Makes roughly 2 litres

1kg langoustines shells, *you can also use lobster or prawn shells*
2 tbsps olive oil
25g butter
1 leek, *roughly chopped*
4 large shallots, *peeled and chopped*
2 tbsps chopped tarragon, *stalks included*
2 tbsps chopped thyme, *stalks included*
300g baby vine tomatoes, *halved*
juice of 1 lemon
2 litres white fish stock, *see page 238*

To make the stock, preheat the oven to 150°C/300°F/gas mark 2. Place the shells in a roasting tray in the oven and lightly roast for about 30 minutes until dried out completely. Meanwhile heat the oil and butter together and sweat the leeks and shallots until softened but not coloured. Add the langoustine shells, the tarragon, thyme, tomatoes and lemon juice and sweat for 10 minutes. Now cover with the stock and simmer for up to 1 hour. Pass the liquid through a fine sieve.

The stock is now ready to use. Allow to cool and refrigerate. It can be stored in the fridge for up to 4 days, or frozen for up to 2 months.

The stock can be easily reduced to make a sauce. Once you have strained the stock, return to the stove, turn the heat up to high, and reduce by half to intensify the flavour. If you add 150ml cream and keep reducing it further it'll make a bisque-type sauce.

SHELLFISH BISQUE

Makes roughly 2 litres

100ml rapeseed oil
1 onion, *peeled and chopped*
2 carrots, *peeled and chopped*
3 sticks of celery, *chopped*
1 bulb garlic, *peeled and grated*
200ml white wine
500g prawn heads and shells, *or langoustine heads and shells*
2 litres white fish stock, *see page 238*
3 star anise
1 tsp fennel seeds
1 tsp coriander seeds
2 tomatoes, *chopped*
150ml double cream
sea salt & black pepper

To make the bisque, heat a large deep-sided pan and add the rapeseed oil together with the vegetables and garlic. Sauté the vegetables without colouring, then add the white wine. Add in the prawn heads and shells and then the stock. Bring to the boil and boil for about 5 minutes, then reduce the heat and simmer for about 15 minutes. Add the star anise, fennel seeds, coriander seeds and tomatoes and continue simmering for about half an hour. Remove the pan from the heat, and remove the star anise. Blitz the liquid slowly in a food processor on a low speed, with the heads and shells included.

Pass the liquid through a fine sieve into another pan. Once you have strained the bisque, return to the stove, turn the heat up to high, and reduce by half to intensify the flavour. Add the double cream, taste and season with salt and freshly ground pepper.

The bisque is now ready to use. Allow to cool and refrigerate. It can be stored in the fridge for up to 4 days, or frozen up to 2 months.

The basics

LANGOUSTINE STOCK —

Langoustines, peanut sauce — 84

SHELLFISH BISQUE —

Lobster ravioli, shellfish bisque — 214

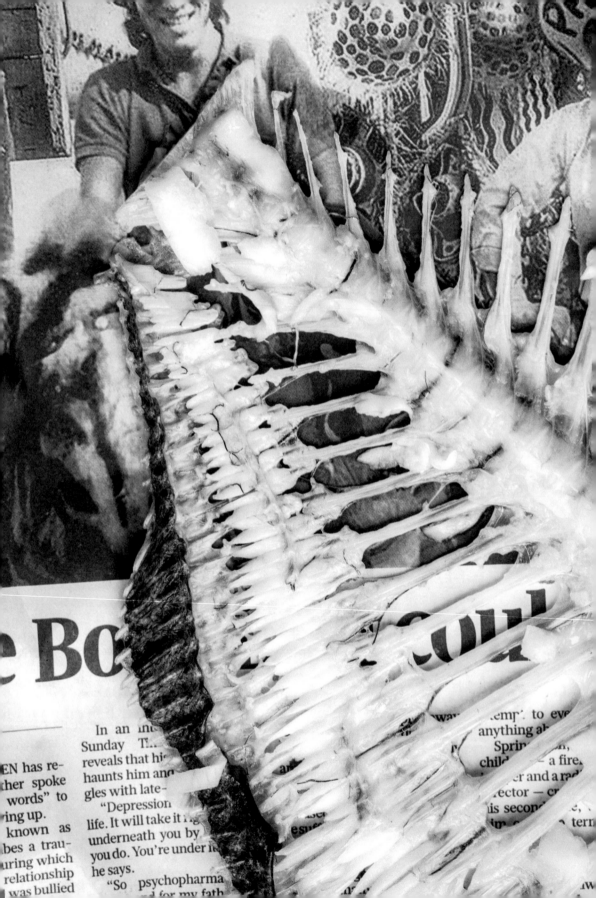

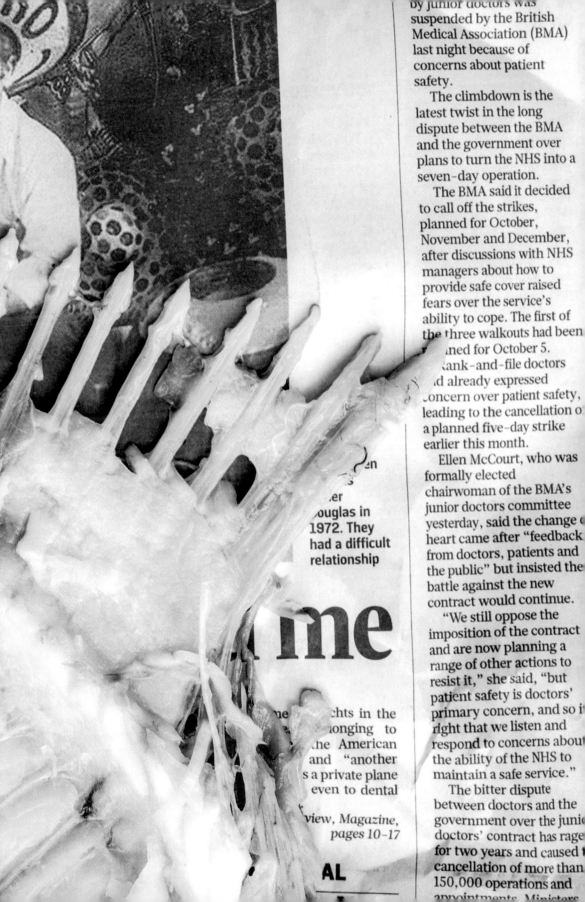

by junior doctors was suspended by the British Medical Association (BMA) last night because of concerns about patient safety.

The climbdown is the latest twist in the long dispute between the BMA and the government over plans to turn the NHS into a seven-day operation.

The BMA said it decided to call off the strikes, planned for October, November and December, after discussions with NHS managers about how to provide safe cover raised fears over the service's ability to cope. The first of the three walkouts had been ...ned for October 5.

...ank-and-file doctors ...d already expressed ...oncern over patient safety, leading to the cancellation o. a planned five-day strike earlier this month.

Ellen McCourt, who was formally elected chairwoman of the BMA's junior doctors committee yesterday, said the change ... heart came after "feedback from doctors, patients and the public" but insisted the battle against the new contract would continue.

"We still oppose the imposition of the contract and are now planning a range of other actions to resist it," she said, "but patient safety is doctors' primary concern, and so i' right that we listen and respond to concerns about the ability of the NHS to maintain a safe service."

The bitter dispute between doctors and the government over the junic doctors' contract has rage for two years and caused t cancellation of more than 150,000 operations and appointments. Minister

...en

...er ...ouglas in **1972. They had a difficult relationship**

...me

me ...hts in the ... ...onging to ...he American ... and "another ...s a private plane ... even to dental

...view, *Magazine*, pages 10–17

AL

OCKLES/COD/CR
CK/HAKE/HALIB
OBSTER/MACKE
PLAICE/PRAWN
SALMON/SARD
A TROUT/SHRIM
SQUID/TURB

*Seafood alphabetically

INDEX*

COCKLES

— Stiffkey Blues: cockles with a distinctive blue shell from mud beds at Stiffkey, just a couple of miles from Morston Hall in Norfolk

HALIBUT

— The largest of all flatfish, halibut is a delicious white-fleshed fish with a firm, meaty texture

Index

MACKEREL —

Grilled mackerel, green bean, fennel
& apple kimchee — 46
Mackerel tart, beetroot & fennel salad — 88

MONKFISH —

Fruity seafood curry — 176
Spiced monkfish, saffron rice — 158

MUSSELS —

Mussel gratin — 90
Mussels, lovage oil & perry — 124

OYSTERS —

Barbecue oysters, chilli dressing — 164
Oyster crackers — 92
Oyster tartare — 48
Southern-fried oysters, pickled cucumber
& dill emulsion — 166

PLAICE —

T-bone plaice with baby squid, champagne
& caviar sauce — 218

PRAWNS —

Crevettes à la plancha — 152
Fruity seafood curry — 176
Galton's fish pie — 202
Haddock, cockle & prawn chowder — 210
Prawn and crab summer rolls, Vietnamese
dipping sauce — 94
Tiger prawn & crab wontons, salad
cream — 96
Tiger prawn & haricot bean soup,
curry oil — 98
Tiger prawn & noodle broth — 170
Tiger prawn & potato curry, samphire
& broad beans — 168
Tiger prawn & potato fritters, Vietnamese
dipping sauce — 172

RED MULLET —

Spicy fish soup, grilled red mullet
& rouille — 154

RED SNAPPER —

Baked whole red snapper, mango
& avocado salsa — 174

SALMON —

Cured blackened salmon, pickled
cucumber — 130
Fruity seafood curry — 176
Galton's fish pie — 202
Salmon ceviche, lime mayonnaise — 126
Salmon & goats' cheese rolls — 128
Seared salmon salad, creamy mayonnaise — 50
Smoked salmon cornets — 56
Smoked salmon, nasturtium pesto
& pressed potatoes — 100
Squid ink crackers with smoked salmon,
lemon purée — 106

SARDINES —

Grilled sardines, seaweed gremolata — 102

SCALLOPS —

Barbecued scallops, chilli dressing — 136
Curried scallops, Gujarati carrot salad — 184
Curried scallops, tomato fondue, samphire,
peaches & chilli pak choi — 140
Fruity seafood curry — 176
Galton's fish pie — 202
Pan-fried scallops, chorizo with spinach
& quails' eggs — 182
Pan-fried scallops, roasted vegetables
& Nantua sauce — 138
Roasted scallops, Sauternes & curry sauce
with cauliflower — 180
Strawberry & lime scallop tartare,
bread crisps — 58

SEA BASS —

Grilled sea bass, champagne & shrimp
sauce — 222
Salt-crusted sea bass, citrus butter sauce — 220
Sea bass, tomato feuilletine & nasturtium
pesto — 60
Tandoori sea bass, ratatouille — 142

SEA BREAM —

Blow-torched sea bream, Sauternes & curry
sauce — 62

SEA TROUT —

Fillet of sea trout, samphire & beurre
blanc — 226
Sea trout ballotine, tomato consommé
& roasted tomatoes — 224
Sea trout & chilli dumplings, Japanese
dipping sauce — 178
Sea trout wrap, mustard vinaigrette — 144

SHRIMPS —

Brown shrimp risotto — 148
Crab & brown shrimp tart — 116
Duck egg with brown shrimps & cockles,
sourdough toast — 146
Grilled sea bass, champagne
& shrimp sauce — 222
Shrimp & spelt batter scraps   — 64

SKATE —

Skate wings, beurre noisette — 228

SOLE —

Dover sole, Café de Paris butter — 200
Lemon sole fingers, Vietnamese dipping
sauce — 42
Lemon sole with Parmesan crust,
asparagus — 120
Slip sole, paprika butter — 230

SQUID —

Salt & pepper squid — 104
Squid in black bean sauce, deep-fried
shallots — 186
Squid-ink-battered halibut, Thai green
emulsion — 188
Squid ink crackers with smoked salmon, lemon
purée — 106
T-bone plaice with baby squid, champagne
& caviar sauce — 218

TUNA —

Bluefin tuna ceviche, Iberico ham, avocado,
melon & roasted tomatoes — 32

TURBOT —

Roast turbot, lemon emulsion with pancetta
& leeks — 232

WHITEBAIT —

Lager, soy & ginger-fried whitebait,
wasabi aioli — 108

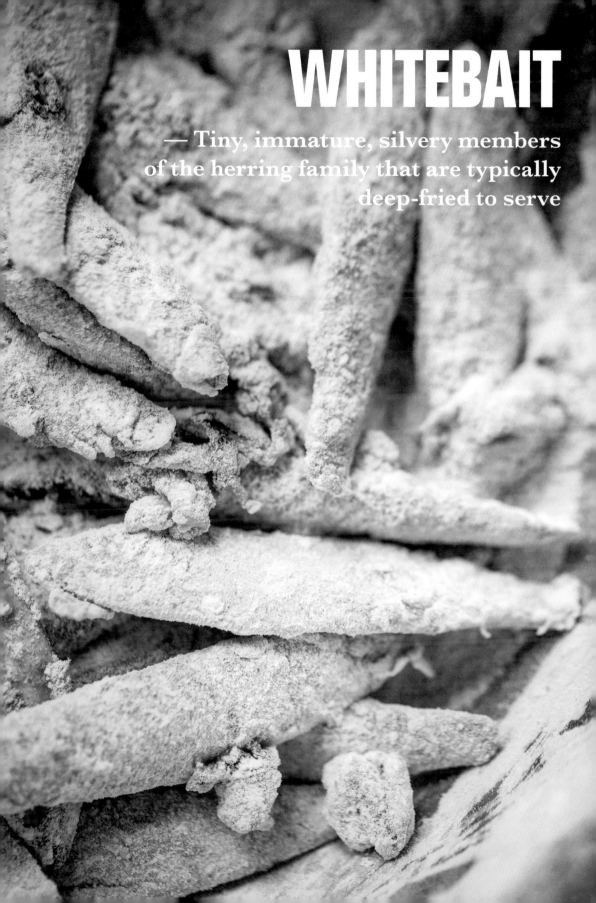

WHITEBAIT

— Tiny, immature, silvery members
of the herring family that are typically
deep-fried to serve

About Galton

Galton Blackiston is one of those chefs who is never content to sit still. He's always looking for new ways to improve Morston Hall, his beloved restaurant and hotel on the north Norfolk coast, where he has been chef patron for 25 years.

With its location a stone's throw from the water, seafood has always been a part of his story and the recent opening of No1, a modern take on the traditional fish and chip restaurant in nearby Cromer, has established Galton as one of the leading seafood chefs in the country.

When he was just 17, Galton ran a food stall on Rye Market selling a range of homemade cakes, biscuits and preserves, known as 'Galton's Goodies', that proved such a success that he would frequently sell out by lunchtime. Realising that his talents lay firmly in cooking, he decided to focus on a career as a chef.

With no formal training, his first job in catering was with the legendary John Tovey at Miller Howe in the Lake District, where he spent four years working in the pastry section gaining creative skills and indulging his love of desserts. He flourished under Tovey's leadership, eventually becoming head chef.

After stints working in London, New York, South Africa and Canada, Galton and his wife, Tracy, set about finding a suitable location to fulfil their dreams. They eventually found Morston Hall, a picturesque flint-knapped farmhouse with 4 bedrooms and a 20-cover restaurant. Since they opened Mortson, it has enjoyed an impressive 22 years in the Good Food Guide, and is widely considered to be a jewel in the crown of Norfolk's up-and-coming food scene. In 1999 the restaurant was awarded a Michelin star, an accolade it has retained ever since.

It's one thing to run a successful Michelin-starred restaurant and retain the star year after year. It's another thing entirely to branch out and open a takeaway, but this sort of challenge makes Galton the chef he is. His great desire is to bring good food to his customers – whether they are gastronomes, or holidaymakers wanting traditional fish and chips.

Galton's seafood dishes have always turned heads. He has a knack of taking simple ingredients and pairing them with techniques and flavours that allow the flavours to remain pure whilst bringing a sense of fun to the occasion.

Hook Line Sinker takes all the fuss out of cooking and gets straight to the point: seafood is incredibly healthy and easy to cook. Galton brings his usual passion and attention to detail to a unique collection of over 90 recipes that has been 25 years in the making.

"MY WIFE TRACY ALON
GREG ANDERSON AND
HAVE ALL PUT UP WITH
HELPED CONVERT MY
INTO THIS BOOK — TH
CUSTOMERS INSPIRED
FIRST PLACE — AND I'D
AND TORI FOR MAKING
THE PHOTOGRAPHY AN
DESIGN AND FOR TAKIN

G WITH MR ALSTON,
JIMMY PRESTON
MY TANTRUMS AND
THOUGHTS AND IDEAS
AT OUR STAFF AND
ME TO CREATE IN THE
LIKE TO THANK JOHN
THIS HAPPEN WITH
ANTHONY FOR HIS
ON THE CHALLENGE"

FIN.